How To Be A Perfect Farm Wife

Reviews

How To Be A Perfect Farm Wife

Lorna Sixsmith

Write on Track Press
How To Be A Perfect Farm Wife
Lorna Sixsmith

Most of the recipes have been handed down or discovered in old cookbooks. They worked for us but you may have to adjust quantities of ingredients or oven temperatures for your own circumstances. Temperatures are given in degrees Celsius for a fan electric oven. For conversion to degrees Fahrenheit or gas mark, please see http://odlums.ie/baking-tips/conversion-charts.

The images for bullets © Bigstock (wellie, bioraven; cooking pot, Microvector; teapot, ratkom)

Published in Ireland by Write on Track
ISBN: 9781518667695

To Brian, Will and Kate

ACKNOWLEDGEMENTS

I'd like to thank all the farmers and farm wives who answered my queries about their own farm lives or helped in other ways: Mary Casey, Gillian Cheatley, Catherina Cunnane, Sarah Jane Drummond, Rebecca Enright, Ailbhe Flaherty, Aideen Fleming, Vicki Flores, Ellen Govern O'Neill, Fiona Graham, Sile Headen, Monica Kearney, Fionnuala Malone McGrath, Elizabeth McDonnell, Bridie Morgan, Ashley Nelson, Donna O'Shaughnessy, Marjorie Quarton, Joe and Ruby Sixsmith, Ann Stenning, Ann Talbot and Leonie Vella. Your assistance was very much appreciated and I hope you all enjoy the read.

Every author needs a proficient and skilled editor. Having a friendly mentor is just as important. I was lucky enough to find both in Sally Vince. Thank you Sally, for your professional expertise and your friendship.

I'd like to thank Joanne Condon for doing the book cover design and interior illustrations, and once again interpreting my instructions so well.

Thank you, Brian, for reading this late at night when you really needed some sleep and for not complaining as I reveal our farming life to readers. Thank you, too, for providing much of the inspiration and fodder for the book! Here's to many more years of farming together.

Thank you, Will, for your sense of humour and infectious giggle, as you make us roar laughing almost on a daily basis.

And to Kate, my wonderful baker, thank you for your scrumptious baking, your patience in helping me find and test the old recipes and for plying me with tea and cakes as I wrote and edited this.

CONTENTS

INTRODUCTION

Born and reared on a dairy and beef farm in Co. Laois, I never imagined that I would be back living here, farming with my husband Brian and seeing my children, Will and Kate, go to the schools I attended, and following in my footsteps for many aspects of their lives. Brian and I worked as a scientist and a teacher for a number of years. We came back to Garrendenny in 2002 to inherit my family's dairy and beef farm. I also teach businesses how to use social media and I ghost write blog posts for businesses too. I never complain of being bored!

My first book *Would You Marry A Farmer?* was inspired by the many responses to my blog post "Ten pieces of advice to anyone considering marrying a farmer". I realised farmers are the same the world over yet are very different to any other occupation. Since its publication, I have occasionally felt like an agony aunt as a number of farmers' wives have asked for advice on various issues, from dealing with their mother-in-law to how to get their husband away on holiday. Some went so far as to state: "Any farmers' daughters I know had way more sense than to marry a farmer." Coming from a different background means many women can feel inadequate, frustrated and isolated living on a farm. They don't necessarily understand the business nor the dynamics in family farming and are left feeling like a "round peg in a square hole". This book is designed to answer some queries presented by farm wives, to show them they aren't the only one in that situation, and to laugh at themselves too.

The traditional Irish family farm was almost always owned by the husband and I have used the term "wife" to reflect on the traditional role within the farming family unit. *How To Be A Perfect Farm Wife* can, of course, apply to the husband of a female farmer or the non-farming half of a same-sex couple. Indeed, women farmers might just be the subject for a future book. While this book reflects on many realistic situations and characteristics, you'll discover the writing is also very tongue-in-cheek.

To all farm wives (and farm husbands), I hope *How To Be A Perfect Farm Wife* provides you with sufficient knowledge to fill you with confidence and help you realise you're pretty darn competent and accomplished after all. If it also makes you laugh out loud, I'll be even happier.

Lorna Sixsmith
Garrendenny, Crettyard, Co. Laois, Ireland.
September 2015

PART ONE

I NOW PRONOUNCE YOU A FARM WIFE

You are married to a farmer. You are now a "farmer's wife". Love it or hate it, that's how many people view you, even if you have another occupation. Some see you as a stay-at-home mum or housewife, others as a businesswoman; some friends might think you are mad for marrying a farmer, and others may be envious of your charmed life in a rural paradise. On occasion, you might be dismissed as "only the wife" by being asked, "Is the bossman around?", although the days of the bank manager considering your off-farm income as pin money have long gone.

Traditionally, most farmers wedded women from similar backgrounds so wives had the advantage of knowing what to expect. They knew there could be long hours, little income and lots of hard work. Marriages are now often between people from diverse backgrounds so some brides just might have a rose-tinted view of living in the countryside on a busy farm.

If your experience of farming before your wedding was visiting your farming uncle and watching *Countryfile* on Sundays, you probably viewed country living as blissful, relaxed, friendly and highly profitable. The sun is usually shining on the televised farm, muck is non-existent, Range Rovers always start on the first attempt, quad bikes are clean, grass is green, corn is golden, new calves and lambs are born without assistance in the middle of the day. The house is a renovated Victorian farmhouse with plenty of character as well as having modern conveniences, and a clean dog is curled up in front of the easy-to-use Aga. You have beautiful views across the countryside and can see three counties on a good day yet the drive to town is only fifteen minutes. Ah yes, you will fit right in, in your checked shirt, denim jeans and clean designer wellies.

I'm sorry to burst your bubble but the reality is very different. The quad is probably third-hand and covered with mud. The dog is a frequent passenger so the seat is mucky too. The tractor is either held together with black silage tape or has a loan the size of a house mortgage. The farmhouse is a 1970s bungalow accessed down a bumpy lane. It rains much of the summer. The cute calf you were about to photograph just had a neighbour poo on his face. Cows calve or sheep break out of their field as you're about to head out on a date.

The road to becoming a perfect farm wife is a long one with plenty of potholes. Although the trappings might not be what you envisaged, there are many benefits to farm life, as you'll find out by reading on. And if you weren't brought up on a farm and feel you're always asking daft questions that cause your new family to roar with laughter, don't despair. The advantage is you haven't developed any bad habits and this book provides comprehensive tips to ensure you become a competent and accomplished farm wife in the easiest way possible.

Love and marriage

Where did you meet your husband? Perhaps you met him at a "young farmers" meeting or an agricultural show. Maybe you knew him many years ago when you were adamant you weren't going to marry a farmer. Perhaps you met him on holidays and you didn't know the first thing about farming.

A century ago, women weren't necessarily able to have a say in their choice of husband. It was even difficult to become a farm wife in the early to mid twentieth century. Women had to have a dowry to marry.[1] Without finance, it wasn't easy to find a farmer who could afford to marry and was willing to wed. In 1911, 25% of Irish women aged 45–57 were unmarried, and in 1936, 44% of women aged 34 were single.[2] People married for land and money, not love. A marriage was often a financial transaction between two families where the bride brought sufficient money or products to compensate for the cost of her future keep and to grant her status in her new home.

H. V. Morton, an English writer travelling around Ireland in the 1930s, was shocked at the lack of romance and the emphasis on matrimony as a business deal.

> She would never know romance as other women know it. Men do not marry for love in agricultural tribes. They marry land or cows or sheep or the potato-patch that runs next to theirs, whichever seems to them the best dowry. There is a proverb in rural Ireland that it is unlucky to marry for love. Scots have a proverb: "As loveless as an Irishman."[3]

Older members (usually male) of the bride's and groom's families, a matchmaker and sometimes the new husband were involved in the negotiations for the dowry. This was still the case until the 1960s in many western areas. In the early to mid twentieth century, it was unlikely all the daughters in a large family would get to say "I do". From a family of six daughters, only two were likely to marry.[4] While the dowry was often a cash amount, usually £100–£250, it sometimes took the form of livestock and furniture. The other daughters emigrated or remained in Ireland as spinsters. Husbands tended to be much older than their wives; many were in their fifties or sixties while their brides were in their late teens to late twenties.

Would you let your father or brother or even a matchmaker choose your spouse? At that time, the bride had very little say in her future. If she declined, her options were limited. If she felt she was too old to emigrate, she could either work as a maid, seamstress or governess, or live with a married brother and his wife and work on their farm.

Peig Sayers (1873–1958) agreed to marry the man proposed by her brother. She could have refused to marry but she wanted her "own hearth" rather than to work as a maid again.

> I was sick and tired of that same service and I thought it would be better for me to have a man to my back and someone to protect me, and to own a house too, where I could sit down at my ease whenever I'd be weary.
>
> My father spoke again: "What have you to say?" he asked.
>
> "I know nothing at all about the Island people", I said "but you know them through and through. Whatever pleases you pleases me and I'll go whenever you tell me."
>
> "God be with you", my father said.
>
> The bargain was made; Peats Guiheen and myself were to be married in a few days' time.[5]

As well as getting her own home, becoming a wife gave women superiority over her unmarried friends and relatives so it was something to aspire to. However, there were other barriers to marital status as social class was very important within the negotiations. A farmer's daughter could marry her equal or better but marrying a landless labourer was totally out of the question.[6]

Religion was critical too and mixed marriages were not tolerated. Many men stipulated the religion within a personal advertisement for a suitable partner.

Irish Examiner 4 December 1948
Respectable farmer's son, Protestant, with sixty acres of land, five miles from Cork, wishes to hear from Protestant girl with view to marriage.

Irish Farmers Journal 12 November 1966
Farm Home is a farmer from Wexford in his late thirties who has a 90 acre well-stocked farm and a nice home and car. He would like to get in touch with sincere C of I girl in her twenties who is interested in farming. He is a non smoker. Strictest confidence given and expected.

Irish Farmers Journal 28 August 1976
UP Kerry is a farmer with two farms who would like to hear from girls (farmers' daughters) with some farming experience. He breeds pedigree Friesian cattle, has own car and lives alone. Would like to meet RC girl with view to marriage. Photo appreciated.

The extent of information required by a potential husband was vast. A writer to a woman's magazine in 1967 was "flabbergasted" when a young farmer on a first date asked her age, occupation, pay and cooking ability, whether she dyed her hair, the cause of her mother's early death, and, significantly, whether she would be able to keep on her job after marriage. Talk about getting the third-degree! Another lady, on a visit to her home place, was asked by a young farmer if her position in Dublin was good enough for her to save for a dowry.[7]

If women were independent and had money of their own, they had some power to choose and many placed advertisements in newspapers. How would you describe your own position? This one from the 1920s reveals an educated professional lady who knows the value of her status in society and the power of her dowry. She clearly has no intention of working hard on a farm and only a gentleman farmer with plenty of staff is going to tempt her.

Irish Examiner 14 April 1926

Lady teacher, dowry £1,100 wishes to meet teacher or other professional gentleman. Merchant or gentleman farmer might suit, would arrange interview.

This advertisement from the 1950s suggests the lady's parents have died recently. She must have been viewed as a "good catch" with her own home and a considerable sum of money.

Irish Examiner 13 August 1951

Farmer's Daughter, 40, Catholic, own home and £700, no encumbrance, wishes to meet gentleman 40 to 50 with view to above. Strictly genuine.

Dowries of that amount were significant and equivalent to the cost of a sizeable farm. Would women these days advertise they have that size of a fortune?

Knowledge about finances was a requirement to attaining wedded bliss and the referencing of dowries in advertisements continued into the 1960s and 1970s. Some women were deliberately vague about the value of their dowry. They weren't necessarily prepared to hand their money over into their husband's possession either. This statement is important as wives had no rights over the family home, even in the 1960s (unless it was registered in both names) and her work counted for nothing. Her home could be sold without her knowledge and consent and she and her children could be made homeless. It wasn't until 1973 that the Social Welfare Act provided for deserted women and unmarried mothers and the children's allowance was paid to mothers.

Irish Farmers Journal 12 November 1966

Dorrinda is a 36 year old farmer's daughter from Kerry who has a good family background. She is kind and sincere, a non-smoker and non-drinker. She would like to get in touch with a farmer of good character. She has a fairly large dowry if required. Strictest confidence given and expected.

Irish Farmers Journal 12 **November 1966**

East Clare Lady is a good looking, well-educated lady in Limerick who would like to meet a refined respectable gentleman with good house and means, with view to marriage. Replies especially welcome from Limerick city, East Clare or Co. Limerick. This lady intends keeping her money in her own name. Strictest confidence given and expected.

As time moved on, the dowry was often replaced by a financial gift from the bride's family. Women earning a good income were seen as a "better catch" by some although others had too much pride to have a wife working off farm.

Women themselves recognised the value of education and qualifications in retaining their independence as well as in the marriage stakes. It was easier for a nurse than a farmer's daughter to marry a prosperous farmer. There were twenty-five nurses in Clogheen, a small parish in Co. Tipperary, in the 1960s.[8]

Irish Farmers Journal 27 **May 1972**

Angus is a farmer in his late 40s (C of I). He owns a large, up to date farm in South Leinster and has good financial resources. He is tall and good humoured, has a good education and varied interests. He wishes to hear from cheerful, sincere C of I lady under 40, who has genuine interest in farm life. Rather tall person with nursing training especially welcome. View to marriage. Photo please.

The following personal advertisement from the 1980s shows that the better-off farmers (dairy farmers in Cork are amongst the wealthiest in the country of course!) were looking out for someone with an income. It wasn't going to be a case of love at first sight.

Irish Farmers Journal **6 February 1988**

Sunbeam is a 41 year old Cork farmer, tall and considered good looking. He has a big dairy farm and a new house and would like to hear from farmer's daughter or nurse in 30–37 age group. Hobbies include hurling, football and country life.

The good news is it's much easier to get hitched to a farmer now – there aren't as many hurdles. You can even marry for love! Mind you, although you don't need a dowry now, it's still useful if you have a good income! There's much to learn and enjoy about being a farmer's wife but it does have its challenges. Thus has it ever been:

Irish Independent **11 Oct 1961**

A Portrait of a Farmer's Wife by John C. Metcalfe

A tanned and hardy soul is she ... The patient, loyal farmer's wife ... who lives out in the countryside depending on the fields for life. The farmer's wife is strong and true ... with golden sunshine in her eyes, a friendly smile upon her face, and in her hair the stardust lies. She toils from morning into night within her house and in the yard ... and there are few in city homes who ever work as long and hard.

If you've been in wedded bliss with a farmer for a long time, you'll be nodding your head as you read on. If you've been married only for a short time, you'll be acquiring this knowledge on a day-to-day basis. If you haven't got the ring on your finger yet, read very carefully.

A family affair

***Irish Press* 15 August 1956**
"Farming is a family business. It is an occupation which demands the contribution and co-operation of all; the farmer, his wife and his children," said Mr Scully. (Author of *The Human Side of Farming*.)

Family farming, even today, means that each person has a role to play in its success: his siblings and parents might also be involved in the operation. When you marry a farmer, you also marry the in-laws, the farm dog and the livestock. You become part of that team even if your experience of farming to date hasn't gone beyond picking out floral wellies for an upcoming festival.

If your father-in-law comments on any part of your anatomy as being useful for the farm, feel pride rather than offence. Your small hands with short fingers might have hindered your playing of the piano but farmers see their worth for helping to deliver lambs. Your muscly arms will mean that carrying buckets of milk will be a doddle. And if you have wide hips, well, the succession of the farm is very safe!

Most families are very close until a disagreement over something farm-related flares up and then tempers can fly or sullen silences last for hours. It could be something hugely important like whether to cut the silage today or tomorrow, or a debate over who left a gate open. The good news is that once the huffing and puffing is over, it all usually blows over quickly.

Before you are let in on the family secrets, remember most lineages have a skeleton in a cupboard or a feud somewhere in the past. Attending weddings or funerals can be somewhat of a minefield as you learn who you should be talking to and who you should be avoiding.

Siblings can feel protective of the farm where they grew up. If you are involved in the farm, they might see you as interfering in their enterprise. If you don't get involved, they may see you as leaving all the work to their put-upon brother. You can't win sometimes. If you are living in the farmhouse (having built another dwelling for the parents-in-law), don't be surprised if out of habit they still walk in the back door without knocking.

The Irish Mammy ("Imagine, she's feeding him rice for dinner!")

All farmers have mothers but Irish farmers have an Irish Mammy! She is devoted to her children, particularly her sons. You are either the apple of her eye or the unfeeling harlot as far as she is concerned. This opinion depends on whether she feels it is time for her son to get married, if the farm needs another woman's touch and the possibility of an heir, and if she is willing to relinquish the role of queen bee. If not, she may see you as a threat to the security of their farm, even accusing you of gold-digging, marrying him for half the value of the farm. Tread carefully if it is the latter.

Her opinion of you also depends on whether you feed him well or let him fend for himself when he gets hungry. The farm wife who works outside the home and encourages her husband to have his midday dinner with his mammy while she cooks another dinner in the evenings is perfect. This ticks both boxes as you're looking after him well and she still feels needed.

He has been brought up on hearty dinners of roast beef, half a saucepan of floury spuds and two vegetables, all smothered in gravy. He hoovers up plain dinners appreciatively. If you prefer "fancy" noodles, pasta or vegetarian food though, he is likely to complain the main course is actually a starter. And never ever try to compete with his mother. Don't ask how your roast dinners or your lovingly made rhubarb crumble compare with hers. No Irish farmer ever wants to be in the position of having to choose between his wife's and his mother's cooking.

In the early to mid twentieth century, the Irish Mammy was a fearsome creature. Many sons were in their 40s or 50s when their fathers died and they inherited the farm. At long last they had the livelihood to afford a wife, but at that stage in life many were loath to cope with a fight for supremacy between wife and mother. Indeed, she was held responsible as one of the reasons for the low rate of marriage amongst farmers.

Daughters-in-law, do remember that once you give birth you are predestined to become an Irish Mammy yourself. Yes, you just might turn into your mother-in-law someday, so maybe cut her some slack.

You'll find out later how to get on with your mother-in-law.

Is it a bit o' road frontage you're after?

Most Irish farmers own the majority of the land they farm. While some rent additional acres, very few Irish farms are tenanted (as is a common feature of British farming). You can truly be mistress of your own domain.

He is passionate about his land; it is as dear to him as his own children will be. Land changes hands only about once every 550 years on average in Ireland compared to every 70 years in France. If you don't like where the farm is, decide how much you really love him as the land is in his soul. Don't make him choose. Each field is named and loved, just like a child. You have to learn their names and yes, you might grow to love them just as much as he does.

Living in the same area, in the same house, within the same community for decades, that's what is normal in farming life. Some people think it is wonderful, others feel claustrophobic. If you are a homebird, you will be happy with the status quo. If you have a touch of wanderlust, you'll find it pretty difficult to achieve long-distance travel (and sometimes even short-distance travel) when you are tied to the farm. Moving the furniture frequently can satisfy the urge for change somewhat – although you may have to wait until your farmer isn't busy before repositioning the heavy dresser and bookcase!

Owning your own farm can also mean you share ownership of a considerable portion of it with the bank. Your wedding guests may think you are sauntering down the aisle with half a farm. You might actually be staggering back down with half of a very large loan.

Isolation or blissful solitude

If your farm is ten miles from the nearest town and two miles up a grass-tracked boreen (as a narrow country road is known in Ireland), you have a choice between viewing it as providing blissful solitude or mind-numbingly boring isolation. For many, it takes time to get used to the quietness and the darkness. There's no roar of cars, no distant hum of voices, no orange hue from street lights at night. The seclusion is wonderful if you love having time to yourself or want peace to write, paint or cook. However, when you find yourself preventing cold-calling salespeople from leaving, you know the isolation might be getting to you and it's time to join a social group.

The farmhouse can be a bit draughty; the wind whistles in the porch and lambasts you as you turn the corner of the house, and the smell of slurry wafts around occasionally. There aren't many windbreaks in the countryside. Whether they are soft breezes or harsh winds, they're certainly effective for getting you going in the mornings. There's no comparison between city fumes and the occasional taint of cow muck.

You truly see the beauty of where you live when people from a city visit, and while they might be aghast at the dirt and manure they are so blown away by the views, the solitude and the feelings of space, you see the wonder of it all again through their eyes. Admittedly, it works best on a warm summer's day.

I'm not going to lie and say a farm life is stress-free. There's the mild anxiety of the annual herd test; the endless arrival of bills; the worry of livestock, grain or milk prices; the concern when animals are sick and at the rapid changes in the weather. But there are also days when you can really appreciate that your commute is a two-minute walk to the yard; you can stop for a few minutes and watch the cows grazing contentedly, the lambs gambolling amongst their mothers or the hens pecking at the grain in the straw shed. You can collect eggs with your small children, take your cold fresh milk from the bulk tank and eat your own produce. There's a lot to be said for the peace and tranquillity of farm life.

The joy of life

Living on a farm means you can really experience and appreciate the changing of the seasons. And by taking photos and sharing them on Twitter or Instagram, you can communicate the beauty to other people too.

January and February bring snowdrops pushing their way out of the cold soil, followed by daffodils and young shoots of corn. March and April see lambs frolicking in fields and cattle racing around with the excitement of getting out of the sheds. May brings lush green grass, trees full of leaf and hedges dotted with hawthorn. June is a busy month for silage-cutting and slurry spreading, creating a patchwork landscape of different coloured fields. The harvests of golden corn, hay and straw fill the senses in July and August; every driver on the road can use the excuse "I got stuck behind a tractor" if late and they'll be believed. September heralds the autumn with hedges full of rosehips and blackberries and church choirs singing out harvest hymns. The trees turn colour in October and create carpets of red and golden leaves. November and December bring some hibernation for farmer and farm as animals are brought indoors, the fields are quiet and bare, machinery is oiled and repaired and the farmer leaves the dark evenings for the warmth of the open fire. Then the cycle starts all over again.

Being married to a livestock farmer means there are plenty of opportunities to see tiny lambs and calves struggling on shaky legs to their mothers' udders. Offspring are usually born without assistance and farmers monitor the situation ready to step in if the mother needs help. No matter how many times you experience watching a newborn suckle, it will always give you a special glow. These are experiences you can enjoy together.

In all aspects of farming, there are bad times to help you appreciate the good ones! You'll be called occasionally at 2am because a calf is coming backwards and you'll work together as a team to deliver it, alive and well hopefully. Sometimes a cow won't take to her calf and will head-butt it around the shed so you have to take it away. A cow may decide to have a lie down, not noticing her tiny calf is under her huge bulk and suffocates it. These occurrences are few and far between thank goodness.

Sometimes a tiny calf or lamb will require special care and this one-to-one feeding usually falls to the farmer's wife. Once you spend hours helping a newborn to recover and thrive, it is always a special one to you.

We had a very special Aberdeen Angus bull calf. Born very early, he wasn't much bigger than a dog and was fed with a baby's bottle. As he grew, he still regularly came up to us for a head scratch. In the end though, as he was male and a beef breed, he had to go to the factory. Brian went to see him in the pen at the factory and he still came over to him for a rub. Brian even contemplated getting the trailer and loading him up to bring him home. It was hard letting him go but that's the lot of the commercial farmer – not to mention the poor bullock.

Sexy farmers?

We are constantly seeing images of male farmers on calendars, billboards and television advertising, looking fit, healthy, attractive and tanned as they promote fresh farm produce. But are they all like that?

Well, there's plenty of physical activity to keep them fit. Feeding calves, bringing in cows, walking up and down a long milking parlour, running after escaped livestock, dosing cattle, fencing,[9] bedding calves and shearing sheep provide them with lots of exercise. On the other hand, consuming two dinners a day, home baking and late night snacks, plus using jeeps and quads rather than Shanks's pony (walking) means he can become portly rather than fit. Keep an eye on the size of those portions!

What about the tanned part? Ireland is more famous for its rain than its sunshine, but his arms, face and neck develop a nice tan as he is outside so much. It stops at the shirt sleeves though. It is known as a farmer's tan as every other part of an Irish farmer's body is likely to be snowy white. As time goes on, he might become rather weather-beaten, but let's describe it as "more rugged"!

It goes further downhill when he arrives in frequently splattered with muck but at least that can be washed off. He could go to the barber more often too! Movember[10] can also happen in March, June and September on a busy farm. But when he does scrub up to go on a night out, the transformation reminds you why you fell in love with him in the first place and you fall for him all over again. Sometimes the huge contrast can be an advantage.

And there will be plenty of potential for your own fitness regime without jumping in a car to go to a distant gym. Instead of running on a treadmill, you'll be racing after livestock, feeding young stock and walking across fields to check on the livestock. The downside is, when you're working hard on the farm, you feel you deserve treats, huge breakfasts and yummy things for a late supper. The farmer is demanding sweet things for his midnight snacks during the calving and yet seems to lose weight. I lose weight every year when I feed 120 calves for two months, but then I forget to cut down on those treats when the calves are weaned! A farm wife needs to reduce her calorie intake during the months when the physical work isn't quite so arduous if she is mindful of her dress size.

If you are out in the elements regularly, you need to decide how your own skin is going to fare. Should you wear sunblock so you eliminate any chance of a farmer's tan? Should you wear fake tan with the sunblock so your skin looks tanned yet is protected? Or will you try to get a fake tan whenever you are wearing a strapless dress to a hunt ball and hope it blends in with your bronzed arms and shoulders? Decisions, decisions.

Ode to a farmer

The Irish are often considered to be poetic. Living in a rural idyll can make an Irish farmer even, well, more descriptive. He never refers to a wet day as just "wet" or "raining". Descriptions include "it's pouring out", "that feckin' rain would cut you sideways", or "it's torrential out there". A perfect farm wife can tell the difference between "driving rain" and "pouring rain" as well as the myriad of other terms we Irish have for liquid sunshine (described later).

You will be exposed to language totally new to you. Sometimes his words have a different meaning to what is in your mind and some will be straightforward. *Yoke* is used frequently and means any implement he can't remember the name of. *Synchronising heifers* may conjure up pretty pictures but means getting them on heat at the same time. *Spending the afternoon drawing cattle* might suggest there's an artist lurking inside him bursting to get out and you visualise him on the hillside with his easel and watercolours. But no, he's heading off to load cattle into a trailer and bring (draw) them to another part of his fragmented farm.

There are also plenty of swear words within his vocabulary, particularly when shouting at his helpers to run faster when livestock break out or when training-in heifers to milk for the first time. Any cows showing signs of unruliness are referred to as "that feckin' hoor". You will pick up these new words pretty quickly once you have joined in a few cattle or sheep chases.

A hard shell with a soft centre

The cynical in society might argue farmers think only of their profit margins. Indeed, he may not appear caring when he is shouting at a wayward sheep, or moaning about a cow being slow to calve as he wants to get to bed (this always makes me wonder if obstetricians grumble about women taking a long time to have babies). After all, I'm pretty sure the cow would like the calf born quickly too.

Farmers hate to lose an animal but they are realists and know an occasional death is inevitable. They hope for the best and can spend hours nursing animals back to health. You know he is caring when he's cradling a tiny lamb in his huge gnarled hands or going out to check a sick calf multiple times during the night. Don't believe him when he tells you his eyes are watering because there's a bit of grit in there.

I remember losing the first cow I fell in love with. I was nine years old and it was the first year I brought the cows in to be milked on my own. Named "The Leader", she was the first cow out of the field and into the milking parlour. I saw her as a huge gentle lady but she was probably just greedy and wanted to be first in to get some nuts. The following year she got milk fever after calving: a serious illness that can affect high-yielding cows. Treatment is an injection of calcium into the vein. Sometimes, they recover; sometimes they die. My dad got the vet to try everything. She was lifted out to the field to see if that would help her get to her feet. She lasted a few more days and I was devastated when I came home from school one day to be told she had gone. I was given her calf as solace and called her Polly. To my disappointment, she was always one of the last in to be milked!

Farmers are a breed all on their own and yet they are similar the world over. They work hard to provide a living for their families, to produce food and to care for their animals and crops. Sometimes they work in challenging weather conditions and have to make hard decisions. They stay strong to the outside world. Under that tough exterior can be a very tender heart. It is distressing when a favourite animal dies but you have to pick yourself up and look after the living.

Romance on the farm

Are farmers romantic? If he brought you flowers when you were dating, you know that tender streak is in there somewhere, perhaps buried deep. And even though you aren't going out for romantic dinner dates during the harvest or calving seasons, you can still head out to work with him on the tractor.

Will he remember your birthday or anniversary? Well, he might remember the tag numbers of his favourite livestock but he isn't always as focused on birthday dates. Where he proposed will tell you much about future chances of romance. It's becoming increasingly popular for men to mark out *Will you marry me?* in their wheat fields, or paint the words on wrapped silage bales, bringing his hoped-to-be-fiancée up in a helicopter to view them. (Imagine saying no after he ruined his field of wheat. It could be dangerous; he could push her out of the helicopter!) Yet, that kind of proposal suggests he will be happy for a romantic anniversary celebration each year.

On the other hand, if he proposes to you at the mart, and then sends you off with some cash to buy the ring on your own, you're unlikely to gain too much in the romance stakes, particularly if he suggests going to the mart cafe every year to celebrate your anniversary.

IS MARRYING A FARMER DIFFERENT?

Years ago, while farmers differed in terms of income, most had mixed farms. They had a variety of enterprises, which often included a few cows, cattle, potatoes, sheep, tillage, pigs and hens, not to mention a garden producing a range of fruit and vegetables. Indeed, in the 1930s and 1940s farmers had to devote a percentage of their land to tillage as it was believed more crops would revive the agricultural sector and Ireland could be self-sufficient rather than dependent on imports. By 1944, all farms over five acres had to devote three-eighths of their farms to tillage.[11] Some were gentlemen farmers with staff. The "strong" farmers had over thirty acres and while they had a workman or two, all members of the family worked hard. Cottiers and small farmers often worked for other farmers or travelled abroad for seasonal labour.

Nowadays, there are fewer farmers, farms are larger and farming tends to be specialised. Farmers have one or two enterprises. Unless the farm is large enough to support a family, farmers often have a full-time off-farm job and farm part-time. Although the enterprises vary hugely from dairy and beef to fruit and vegetables or from sheep to mushrooms, the farming way of life tends to be similar. Yet, it is very different to the lifestyle of any other occupation. Let me explain.

His & hers

When we were working as a teacher and scientist, we shared the housework pretty evenly. Brian cooked dinners; I did the cleaning and washing up. While he washed windows, I ironed the clothes. Most couples who are employed seem to share the household tasks. It can be quite different in farming, depending on the type of enterprise and the size of the farm. If both of you are working on a busy farm, it is usually the wife who cooks the vast majority of the meals, mops floors, washes dishes, hangs out clothes, puts out the bins, hoovers the rooms and cleans the bathroom. It's a rare farmer who washes up or takes turns cooking the meals. If you have one of those, hold onto him tight!

An occasional farmer even expects his work clothes to be ironed. I'm not sure if it is his common sense or lack of courage, but my husband wouldn't dare request such a thing.

In the past, farming roles were divided even more: men worked in the fields while women did the housework and yard work. The contrast between urban and rural wives then was: the city wife cooked and cleaned, the country wife looked after the house *and* the animals. Yes, the city wife was expected to have the house tidy, children washed, make-up on, dinner cooked and be ready and waiting to listen to stories of his day in the office. At least the farm wife didn't have that pressure!

Men worked late during the busy months of sowing and harvesting but they could stop when the horses got tired. Once they went into the house in the evening, their work was finished. They didn't change nappies or rock babies to sleep; they didn't carry water or do any housework. Many went to the pub in the evenings for a pint, a chat and some relaxation. Others sat by the fire and read the newspaper or listened to the radio. When women sat down at the fireside at night, it was rare their hands were idle as they sewed, knitted jumpers or darned socks.

This letter (I presume the writer was female) emphasises the amount of work completed by farmers' wives in the course of a day:

Irish Independent 31 January 1935
Letter to Editor
Farmers' wives with young children are the silent sufferers.

She commences by lighting the fire, going out to milk, then returns with the milk perhaps of 3 or 4 cows, then she has to prepare breakfast for often as many as ten, get ready for school six or seven children, 2 or 3 more not yet of school-going age, they also have to be looked after. She has to continue the drudgery through the day and at least 20 or 30 more meals have to be prepared. There is no money to pay anyone to help her with the work.
Advocate of the Downtrodden

Women's farm tasks included feeding smaller and young animals such as calves, lambs, pigs and poultry. They also fed men, made butter, cured meat and baked bread. Buckets and churns had to be kept clean too. Most of these women had large families, many having between six and ten children. As one interviewee reminiscing on her early days of marriage said: "We didn't have time to think about morning sickness; we just got on with it."

At one time women were the main milkers of cows, but as mechanisation was introduced from the 1940s and cow numbers increased, milking became more popular amongst men. It came to be seen as a "man's job" and all the milk went to the co-ops. What's more, payment from the co-ops came once a month with the cheque made out to – no surprise here – the farmer. When women controlled the milking, they made butter to sell to shops or at the market for much-needed income.

As time went on, and the amount of paperwork in farming increased, women took on that role as well as taking care of the house, looking after pet lambs, feeding calves, washing dairies and keeping hens. One significant change for women was the removal of the marriage bar in 1973,[12] so women could continue working in public sector careers after getting married. Some farmers didn't like the idea of their wives working, believing others would see it as a necessity rather than choice (that he wasn't "able to afford to keep her"). The Irish Countrywomen's Association (ICA) opposed married women working outside the home, although they were keen to promote crafts, the provision of holiday accommodation and other businesses within the farmstead.

Mrs Oonagh Corbett, President ICA 1970–72

I am not in favour of wives working for the sake of purchasing luxuries in the home. The greatest luxury should be the home environment and the wife or mother plays a vital part in establishing that.

There must be something wrong if a mother has to take up a job because she feels bored with being in the house.[13]

As you can see, within the heritage of farm families, the roles were quite segregated. Times are changing and many young farming couples share the workloads more evenly. He puts out the bins and clears the table and she helps with the milking. He shares the childminding by taking a youngster out on the farm to check the cattle or on the tractor for a few hours. He's happy to push a pram or change a nappy. He may not fix that loose skirting board for months but he is around if you need him. Reading stories to children, mopping the floor, clearing the table: it all means a lot when you've been looking after small children all day. He appreciates the help and the company on the farm too.

Bob the Builder

Farmers often believe they are capable of turning their hands to almost anything, be it carpentry, painting, wallpapering, putting up shelves, fixing loose skirting or replacing a light fitting. They insist on doing these jobs rather than paying a decorator, carpenter or plumber. Yes, they *can* do all those odd jobs (although, *ssshhh*, perhaps not as well as a professional) but the challenge is in pinning him down to do them. He's more inclined to find a farm job that needs doing than to put up a shelf for you.

You want to hang up new curtains and they need a new pole. He says not to bother calling in a handyman or a curtain fitter, he can do it easily. Between waiting six months for him to do it and then having an argument as he discovers the ceiling isn't straight and the pole looks crooked, you wonder if secretly paying the professional might have been the best option.

Brian is quite good at wallpapering and I enjoy painting so we make a good decorating team. But now that he is a farmer, he helps out with those jobs only in December and January. Between relaxing over Christmas, taking a holiday in January and getting ready for the calving, it leaves very little time for decorating. Once the cows start calving, it will be another ten months before I can coerce him to do any more. Marrying a farmer doesn't mean he can't be a handyman or decorator; it's just the window of time for those tasks is very narrow.

We all know the jokes about men disappearing into their garden sheds for hours at a time (those times often being when there are domestic jobs to be done). Yes, the farm is like one giant men's shed, so the hours can turn into days. Even if he didn't have to work long hours, he would probably be out there tinkering around in any case. The advantage is he will never be under your feet with the farm as his shed.

"Does my bum look big in this?"

Whatever about the torture of bringing any man shopping for an afternoon, I'd really recommend leaving a farmer at home. He will be amazed at the cost of food in the supermarket (and complain constantly that farm incomes aren't increasing) and will be shocked at the price of the dresses you try on. If you really want his opinion on an outfit for a special occasion, buy it when on your own, making sure you can return it. If you decide you might like to try clothes shopping as a nice day out, go only to shops with seating areas and newspapers for non-shopping partners.

I'd equate it to a day in purgatory though. All you will hear all day is, "Sure, haven't you loads of clothes," and "Sure, that black pair of shoes you have will go grand with it." And don't even dream of asking him "Does my bum look big in this?" as you don't really want to hear his reply.

If he needs new clothes, "nip" in to a clothes shop for half an hour when you are out for Sunday lunch and get it done and dusted quickly, before he realises.

Before we returned to farm, we often did the supermarket shopping together and he used to do it on his own too. Brian is in a supermarket twice a year now at most. When the children were little, we went on holiday to Cork and it was a huge treat for them to have him shopping with us. As one of their favourite books at the time involved twins going to the supermarket with their parents, they felt they were living the story. That is what life is like with a farming dad – going grocery shopping with him is hugely memorable.

Hell's Kitchen

It is rare that a farming husband is willing and able to cook some of the meals. Some will clear the table or unload the dishwasher but even that can be very sporadic. On a positive note, at least they don't criticise the way you stack it (as some non-farming husbands allegedly do – surely life is too short for such criticism?). My friend was pleasantly surprised to see her husband had unloaded the dishwasher, until she opened it and found some freshly washed tractor parts in there!

People working away from home tend to have their dinner in the evenings, relaxing with a cup of tea afterwards while watching a soap opera. Many farm families have their main meal at one o'clock with a "high tea" in the evenings. Eating a big meal so early would probably send office workers to sleep; farmers often need that protein hit to keep their energy up for the rest of the day.

Our dinner time is 3:30 when the children get home from school. Brian still manages to be late even though his post-milking breakfast was hours earlier. Reasons include something going wrong or being delayed by a caller. Sometimes he finishes working and decides to fit in another job that should take twenty minutes but ends up taking an hour.

If I've been away, he knows dinner will probably be late so he texts asking "What time is dinner?" and I'll reply with "3:45", aware it will be 3:55 by the time the potatoes have boiled, but guessing he will be late anyway. He doesn't arrive in until 4:05 knowing I'm never accurate with time.

Of course, now I have put this in writing, he knows my secret. Dinner will be at 4:30 before long.

The main thing is to cook dishes that can be kept warm and use the time you're waiting for him to do something worthwhile, like catch up with your friends on Facebook.

Blowing a fuse

If you both work in different jobs, you won't be seeing each other enough during the day to argue too much. If you are working together on the farm, you have plenty of time to bicker and get antsy.

You might both be angling for an argument because the weather isn't playing game or a silly calf stepped on your foot and you want to take the pain out on someone. The beauty of farming is you can use the situation to let off some steam. Working with livestock means something is bound to go wrong – have you heard the expression, "never work with animals or children"? There's a reason for that – and you can swear at each other with gusto. You know it's really the fault of the calves or sheep for all looking so similar or not being in exactly the right spot.

The reality is you can use farming to blow that fuse, and being a perfect farming couple you know never to take those insults personally.

We're all going on a ... ~~holiday~~ day out

Farming can mean viewing that overnight trip to a sheepdog trials or to view a pedigree animal as the annual family holiday. When I look back on the paid time off we used to get, I wish I had appreciated it more! Brian got 32 days paid holiday a year plus bank holidays. I got the UK teachers' holidays of about thirteen weeks, and at that I felt envious of Ireland's teachers with their longer summer holidays.

Of course, being married to a farmer means he is self-employed and you can both take a day off whenever you want. There is just the small matter of arranging for someone else to check the animals and milk the cows. If family or staff are available to cover, that makes it much easier. However, some farmers don't like going away and leaving their livestock, after all, someone else might not be able to milk them as well as they do. Farmers enjoy farming and they can prefer it to a day out. Keep it secret, but they have been known to claim that cows are calving so they can leave social situations early.

If your new husband spent considerable time on honeymoon angling to visit a mart or "combine spotting" as you drove down American highways, that hints at what any future holidays might entail. Never fall asleep while he is driving as you might wake up to find yourself in a farmer's yard, having just been invited on a tour of the farm. If you find yourself pointing out good grass to girlfriends when on a day trip away with them, you realise it's now a family trait.

As a child, the closing music of *Glenroe*[14] always signalled that back-to-school feeling. When we were PAYE employees, Sunday evenings meant ironing clothes for the week. On a farm, the days blend into each other with the exception being a few hours off on a Sunday afternoon. Cows and goats require milking, livestock need to be fed if indoors, animals outdoors have to be checked, eggs need collecting, it's all hands to the deck if the harvest needs to be brought in and rain is forecast. As a farmer, you never have that Sunday night/Monday morning dread but you don't necessarily get that Friday "yippee" feeling either.

But if the sun is shining on a Wednesday morning in June, the silage is in and fertiliser is spread, he might text from the milking parlour with: "Let's go to the beach. I'll be ready by 10:30." You still won't leave any earlier than 11:30, but sometimes a little sunshine can create some spontaneity so grab it with both hands and prepare a picnic. Getting an unexpected day away, especially if it is a week day, makes you appreciate it all the more.

As the expression goes, if you work at something you love, you won't work a day in your life – but time off, particularly if unexpected, recharges those batteries beautifully.

Desperate Farmwives

Many town and city dwellers don't know most of their neighbours, whereas a farmer usually lives on the same farm all his life so he is familiar with every family in the area not to mention their past history for generations.

Everybody knows nearly everyone in country locations; they know what families are related by blood or marriage, when they were born, where they were educated, their religion, their farming skills, when they last went on holiday, if they are good bakers, what car they drive and the name of their dog.

People in farming communities like to know what is going on and it is very difficult to keep something a secret. They won't ask questions outright, nor will they quiz just one person. Instead they pretend to be disinterested but will ask various people different questions so they can come up with the full picture ... or *a* full picture.

Having said that, having good neighbours is invaluable; your neighbourhood watch means someone will telephone if they spot your livestock out, stand in a gap if they happen to be there when you're moving cattle, or arrive with food when there's been a calamity. That's worth being gossiped about. Isn't it?

Air kisses or the wink

The farmer method of greeting people can take them by surprise. Most people greet others with a nod and a "good afternoon". Kisses on both cheeks may be exchanged. Apart from the fact that the average farmer isn't overly comfortable with air kisses, it's best to ensure he has showered before visitors invade his personal space.

Farmers acknowledge others with "the farmer wink". This is comprised of one eye closing and opening quite slowly with a swing of the head at the same time. A slurred "howareye" will be emitted too.

Many years ago, when helping me collect the wedding cake, our best man thought he was being chatted up by another customer in the bakery, but no, it was just a friendly farmer saying hello and winking, as they do.

Ah, go on, you'll have a cup, sure, the kettle is on

If you are used to city life, you are probably accustomed to no meaning no. If someone offers you tea and you say no, they usually accept that you don't want a cup of tea. If you said "no" from politeness, expecting them to offer again, you're left feeling disappointed and thirsty. If you say yes, you get just that – a cup of tea, with a biscuit if you are very lucky. No cake, no homemade tart, no scones.

If you say no to a cup of tea in rural Ireland, you are asked another couple of times and the kettle is put on anyway, confident in the knowledge you will change your mind (whether you want to or not). If biscuits are the only thing on offer, they come with apologies. There is likely to be a choice of homemade cakes if your visit is expected.

A true farmer's wife is capable of wielding a huge teapot at any event, pouring copious cups of tea and she believes "a grand strong cup of tay" to be the cure of all ills. Just don't ask her for coffee.

The farm is in his blood

Most employed people have a private or public pension with their job, maybe the added benefit of health insurance too. Of course, being employed means there is always the risk of redundancy, but retirement for most brings a comfortable income and if they have downsized their house, extra income from that.

Farmers are often so busy making repayments to the bank and educating their children that pension planning isn't top of the list. When retirement comes, most pass the farm to one of their children. If their pension isn't big enough, they hold onto some land and rent it to the succeeding farmer. They usually stay living on the farm too, either in the farmhouse or in the bungalow the younger farming couple has built for them nearby. It is rare an older farmer ever really retires in this situation; he will still help out.

Some years ago, a condition of getting income from an early retirement scheme was not being on the farm. While this scheme encouraged transfers to younger farmers and enabled them to farm independently, it really didn't recognise how farming gets into people's blood. They might as well lose a limb as not farm. Once they retire, they enjoy not having the responsibility and the stress, but still love to be involved in the work, seeing grandchildren out and about and being able to help out when they feel like it.

If there is no successor, the older couple face a choice of selling up, leasing out the farm, setting up a partnership with a young farmer, or continuing to farm themselves. Most farmers find it very difficult to sell their land. They may change to a less intensive and more easily managed system of farming, but they'll continue it on.

A farmer stays a farmer until he is six feet under.

Does his wife stay a farmer's wife for that length too?

WHAT IS A FARM WIFE?
WHAT DOES SHE DO?

Irish proverb: A man's work is from sun to sun,
but a woman's work is never done.

In the past, a farm wife worked alongside her husband. It is unlikely she was employed elsewhere although if living in the West of Ireland, he may of financial necessity have worked abroad for months at a time, leaving his wife to keep the farm going. She was often the backbone to the business, ensuring there was a steady income, children were fed and educated, and sometimes keeping a husband on the straight and narrow too.

Irish Independent 1963[15]
In the farmhouse kitchen a woman is up to her elbows in a bucket of mash, a baby yells blue murder from a pram, a toddler on the floor trying to find nourishment in a sod of turf while strangling the cat. Somewhere outside a chorus of hungry hens is squawking like teenagers at a pop concert and from the yard "himself" is shouting for details of the clown who let out the cows. The woman says "God, give me patience", looks at the clock and wonders if she should try to feed the hens before settling the baby, before

starting the dinner for the children at school. She is wife, mother, cook, needlewoman, nurse and gardener.

What is a farm wife nowadays? Many women marrying farmers don't realise the amount of work and level of science that goes into farming. You might suppose sheep become pregnant after a romantic liaison, whereas the ram is specifically chosen by analysing different traits. You might presume grass grows by itself, the cows provide the milk and the farmer rakes in the money, but there's plenty of work and research in choosing the best grass seeds, spreading fertiliser at the correct times, measuring grass and breeding the best cows for milk quality and fertility. Crops don't just grow for six months once planted in the ground, they need plenty of attention too. Of course, if you answered a personal ad stating "help wanted milking cows", you knew what you are getting into and are well prepared for the work load!

The job description for a farm wife is extensive. You are expected to be an expert cook, keep the home comfortable and spotless 24/7, rear young livestock, be great in bed, stop gaps, milk cows, drive tractors, reverse trailers, be patient, nurture your husband and children, look equally good in wellies or heels, bring in additional income, be fit enough to run past escaping cattle and turn them around, keep paperwork up to date and have the foresight to plan ahead for almost every eventuality. Okay, maybe not quite all of those are expected for you to achieve perfection, but failing on any just might be emphasised by certain people with jealous tendencies. You'll be a hired hand without pay but you will have job security!

How do you describe yourself when asked what you do? Some women use the term "housewife" even though they have their own business on the farm, be it providing accommodation for tourists or selling eggs for many years. Some describe themselves as a "farmer's wife" and often downplay the amount of work they do on the farm, feeling others would look down on them. Others understate it because they don't want their husbands to feel inadequate. Maybe it is because farmers who could afford a workman (while the wives concentrated on the home) held more social status in the past?

While some farmers take their wife's hard work for granted, others notice and appreciate it. It is not unusual to hear farmers describing another farmer's wife in glowing terms, such as "She's a right woman, you'd see her out milking cows and feeding calves", or "She'd do the work of a man". If the husband is lazy, she will be commended with "Sure, she keeps the place going." Working hard means receiving admiration, often by men who wish they had as capable and hardworking a wife. Heaven help you from the gossipers if you're deemed to be lazy though.

Strangely enough, the fairer sex can sometimes be each other's worst enemy and some women look down on others who work hard on the farm as though being employed or a "yummy mummy" has more status. Being a farm wife is much more complicated than it might initially seem!

What is a farmer's wife?

Is the farmer's wife a housewife or a business manager, an assistant or an equal? Some people use the term "farmer's wife" to insinuate being an assistant rather than a valuable half of the team. Yes, there are farming couples where the wife is given her housekeeping money and has no say whatsoever in the farm spend or the business. There are also couples where the wife usually deals with all of the finances and decisions are made jointly, or she is the decision maker.

I think it is important not to view paperwork, cooking, collecting parts and delivering food as mere assistance. They may be chores rather than skills (although I'd argue that as well), but they are none the less crucial to the success of the business. Many American farmers' wives especially are proud to be called a farmer's wife and consider it a description of an essential role. Farmers work on their stomachs and need good food; it is important someone provides it.

Farmers' wives are runners, collectors, managers, tractor drivers, cooks, nurses, bookkeepers, IT specialists, child-minders, mediators, supporters, seamstresses, homemakers, cleaners, shoppers, teachers, probably mums, bakers, and maybe even butchers and candlestick makers!

Just as a chef running a restaurant needs staff or family to help in the kitchen, run front of house and take bookings, the farming family is a team, all with their important roles. In the past it was the case that "behind every great man (farmer) was a great woman (farm wife)". Stand up beside him and see yourselves as equal partners in a thriving business.

Whether you are employed full-time or part-time off farm, working on the farm or helping out, remember farming is more than a full-time job. Managing to spend time together, sharing the workload, ensuring income exceeds outgoings so you can save for a rainy day, this all takes teamwork and some delicate negotiation too. Running a business, especially if you become parents, means there are times in the year when both of you are exhausted and find it difficult to relax. All work and no play means life can become drudgery so find some ways to spend quality time together, both on the farm and on an occasional day out.

What is a *perfect* farm wife?

What exactly does a farm wife have to do to be considered the ideal farm wife? That can vary according to different people's perspectives. There are certain skills that are expected and others which represent the cherry on top of the cake.

From the **farmer's perspective**, a farm wife is perfect if she can be all or most of the following:

A domestic goddess

◢ Cook hearty meals of meat, potatoes and two vegetables followed by a filling dessert and a pot of tea. Being able to cook for contractors without complaint is appreciated too. Always serve with a smile.

◢ Bake cakes and bread that are almost as good, if not better, than his mother's (although it will be a brave man that will tell you so). Be particularly prolific during the calving/lambing season.

◢ Make the dinner taste just as good if he's in thirty minutes early or two hours late.

◢ See bringing dinner to him in the field as a good idea especially when it is a long way from the farmhouse and he's trying to finish ploughing/sowing/harvesting before the rain comes. Especially without getting lost.

◢ Be able to kill, pluck and clean out birds for the table.

◢ Be content with drinking whole milk fresh from the bulk tank – he won't tolerate semi-skimmed or soya milk in the fridge ("It's just water!").

Financially canny

◢ Bring in a salary, particularly during the lean months when the farm doesn't have an income.

◢ Be good at budgeting money and managing cash flow. Remain calm about the fact there's no farm income for some months of the year.

◢ Remain calm when the money you have earmarked for a holiday or a new bathroom is spent on a new slurry spreader. Whoever said "where there's muck, there's brass" anyhow?

◢ Be innovative. It has been proven that women in farm families are more inventive than the men. They think outside the box, take calculated risks, aren't as nervous about what the neighbours might say, and are often more sociable so don't mind going to farmers' markets to test the market with their new product. If you can create a product that adds value to the farm produce, it really will be the icing on the cake.

⊿ Be thrifty by upcycling and recycling. Try to live a sustainable lifestyle by growing your own vegetables and fruit, and perhaps even produce your own meat, milk, cheese and yoghurt.

Wonder Woman

⊿ Produce an heir and a spare for the farm. Note I said "the farm". Succession is important and if the children are hugely interested in farming, it is usually considered to be a bonus.

⊿ Be telepathic. An example is knowing instinctively that he means you to feed the sheep today when he points and grunts.

⊿ Be good at orienteering and understand exactly what he means when he says "the field to the right of the top field which is beside the round field beyond the Quarry Field".

⊿ Be an optimistic soul and see every cloud as having a significant silver lining so you can cheer him up when things are tough.

⊿ Know how to drive a tractor. If you can reverse a trailer, that's a big bonus.

⊿ Dip sheep and feed calves. And be happy to take over the calf and pet lamb rearing on your own. If you are strong enough to carry buckets of milk and see it as an effective way of keeping fit, he'll be even more pleased as it will save him the cost of a quad and milkbar feeder.

⊿ Keep hens. Given the heritage of farmers' wives and their hens, you have to keep poultry. Even just four will provide the house with sufficient eggs.

⊿ Not be squeamish when he needs your help at the rear end of an animal. Having a spare pair of gloves in your pocket is a good idea. If he actually tells you that you need gloves, you know it is going to be really disgusting.

⊿ Be vigilant with health and safety. Farmers tend to be so engrossed in tasks, they are often too close to be able to stand back and assess the dangers. He might complain when you make him do the safety assessment document, ensuring that possible dangers are identified and fixed, but he knows he won't do it unless he is nagged!

⬛ Be able to use baler twine for multiple uses – thereby saving money! Understand how it can be used to secure a fence, light a fire, repair a broken halter, act as a belt on your trousers, be an emergency lead for dogs or horses, fasten a gate and tie a trailer shut. (More on this later.)

⬛ Above all, have a sense of humour. Be capable of making him laugh when crying is the only alternative.

And be Superwoman

⊿ Organise the filing and accounts so he doesn't have to worry about paperwork or dealing with the accountant.

⊿ Never throw out a copy of his favourite farming paper until he has read it cover to cover (and possibly not even then).

⊿ Find the important scrap of paper (complete with scribbles) he left on the table three days ago.

⊿ Organise his wardrobe so he can find co-ordinated "good" clothes easily. While you might have only half an hour to get ready, he is usually limited to ten minutes. He doesn't want to embarrass you so it's just easier if you advise him on what to wear.

⊿ Pair his socks and organise them into good socks, work socks and extremely cold-weather socks.

⊿ Multi-task. Looking after children, cooking meals, keeping an eye on a calving cow, answering the telephone – and all at once – shouldn't stress you at all!

⊿ Comply with all regulations – from knowing how much fertiliser you can spread, to keeping records of all animals born and recording any deaths.

Be so relaxed you're almost horizontal

⊿ Although you're expected to be efficient, he doesn't want you nagging him either, so never tie him down to an exact time for anything. Don't pester him if he doesn't get in for dinner on time or forgets to do that one job you asked him to do. It may be infuriating, but there are always emergencies that take precedence on a farm.

⊿ Be capable of entertaining yourself during the busy season. This can be interpreted as going out to work with him, starting your own business, or seeing your friends regularly. He doesn't mind as long as you aren't tormenting him with requests to finish work earlier because you are lonely. Don't be tempted to say that "Xxx's husband is able to finish early". You never know, that husband might be nagged to within an inch of his life or they have more help on the farm.

⊿ Look good in wellies as well as heels. He would love you to know all about the farm so that he can discuss decisions – which cows to cull, which bulls to use, whether to show a sheep at the agricultural show, what crops to sow – but he also likes that you scrub up well, just as you like him to spruce up when required.

⊿ He will be as frustrated and disappointed as you when attempts to head off on a night out are thwarted, so it'll be appreciated if you remain calm and relaxed.

Bear in mind, a woman who can achieve all this is unlikely to exist, but a few do come close! Don't worry though, having the managerial skills to delegate is important too and I'll be showing you how you can do just that as you read on.

The perfect farm wife according to the in-laws

- Produce an heir and a spare.
- Be able to feed the farmer nourishing and hearty dinners so he can keep his strength up.
- Create a meal in minutes if contractors or visitors arrive unexpectedly.
- Help out with various community events (their family was always heavily involved and they don't want you letting the side down).
- Bring in an income yet be free to go and collect tractor parts if necessary.
- Ensure the farmer and the children are smartly turned out for all off-farm outings.
- Keep the house and garden tidy.
- Be hardworking and never stay in bed later than 8am.
- Never leave clothes hanging out for more than two days.
- Be able to drive a tractor, feed calves and deliver lambs – in fact, take the place of a workman.
- Be a good baker (but not, of course, as good as your mother-in-law).
- Be thrifty and certainly not spend "his" money on "unnecessary" modern conveniences or lots of new clothes.

There is a limit to how well you should do all this though. It's a fine line between doing it well enough to be seen as good enough and yet you don't want to surpass your mother-in-law's abilities.

Don't be scared, you will be working as a team – it's not all down to you. This might seem like a long list but read on to discover how you can achieve these accomplishments and, more importantly, what you can get away with!

PART TWO

FARMING RELATIONSHIPS

A family farm is a busy place. Whether it is the two of you or an extended family working on the farm, everyone wants to have their say. Farmers don't tend to bother too much with roles or job descriptions, AGMs or regular weekly meetings. There's lots of scope for stepping on each other's toes, but this section shows you how to stay on good terms with family members, have a great relationship with your farmer, enjoy the rural life with your children, use your existing skills to advantage on the farm and, above all, stay safe.

HOW TO "MANAGE" YOUR FARMER

Farmers can be unpredictable at times. They can be very different to others in "normal society". Your friends and their husbands may look askance occasionally at your lifestyle, at his clothing, at the hours he works. Whether you want to blend in or stand out, here's how to manage your farmer in certain social situations.

How to go on regular dates with your farmer

Before you married, he probably made a good effort to go out on dates. He might have arrived late, with damp hair, smelling strongly of aftershave and with a ready excuse of how the latest mishap on the farm delayed him, but he *did* endeavour to go out.

For your first date, you may have dressed in high heels and a sexy top, expecting to be going to a nightclub but ending up feeling overdressed (or, rather, underdressed) at a young farmers' club where everyone else was wearing jeans, shirts and boots. Does that ring a bell?

You had the chance to run when you looked around and realised he saw this as a perfect night out!

After the wedding, courtship rituals become a dim and distant memory as the busy days and nights of farming take over. There are many months in the year when he is too busy to commit to a night out. Even family weddings requiring his attendance are greeted with a "maybe". All proposed nights out receive an "I'll see" unless he knows he might face divorce proceedings if he fails to do something for a special occasion. If you're all dressed up to go out and you dissolve into tears when he comes in with news that there's a cow calving, you know you have to be creative and view time on your own with him, on the farm, as a distinctive kind of date.

Don't wait for him to finish work. Put on the wellies and head out with him. There's nothing as romantic as a walk across a flower-strewn meadow on a sunny day to check on the livestock. You could bring a picnic to make it feel like a date. But make it clear this is a way of spending time with him or he is likely to suggest you learn how to do that job on your own in future!

The passenger seat on the tractor is there for a reason. Admittedly, it is not the most comfortable if he is driving on a bumpy track or field, but you can sing along to the radio as he drives against the backdrop of the sun setting a deep red on the horizon.

How to manage a sleepy husband when visiting friends

There are various times of the year when both of you are sleep deprived and it's difficult to visit friends or go out. As you are likely to be the chauffeur, it's important you get sufficient sleep

to stay awake when driving, so never ever feel guilty about rolling over for another hour's sleep when he gets up at the crack of dawn to milk the cows.

You become accustomed to his snoring at night, not to mention the numerous alarm clocks that go off every morning. Once you can sleep through them all, you know you're an established farm wife! You're used to him falling asleep at the kitchen table, sometimes mid-sentence, although it may take longer to adjust to the fact that he can resume a conversation perfectly after a fifteen-minute power nap. But what about when you're visiting people and he falls asleep in an armchair? Will they think it's rude?

Having a nap while you are driving means he should stay awake for part of the evening. Once he's eaten, though, tiredness sets in again. Men are hopeless at hiding yawns. While you can manage a grimacing smile while yawning with your mouth closed, or pretend to let something fall to the floor and yawn sneakily while retrieving it, he finds it impossible (does he even try?).

If you are visiting farmers, they will understand when he falls asleep and indeed, some of them might have a quick snooze too, but if you are staying with "townies", they won't necessarily recognise the need for sleep and might be offended.

If he does fall asleep when you're out visiting, suggest a stroll to keep him awake, or sit beside him and kick him repeatedly on the ankle. Alternatively, you could be considerate and let him sleep to his heart's content. As long as he doesn't snore, his sleeping won't affect the conversation and if he is in a comfy armchair by the fire, he will wake feeling blissfully refreshed after his power nap.

How to ensure the perfect gift from your other half

If you want to receive a particular present, start planning now. Left to his own devices, your dearly beloved is likely to pick up something at the local creamery or hardware store. It might even come with the receipt attached so he can claim it as a tax-deductible expense.

I rarely receive a Valentine's Day gift as we're always busy with calving in February, but this year, Brian spotted what he considered to be the ideal present. When he told me he'd purchased it at the creamery, I presumed it was a new calf feeder (I've learnt not to have high hopes!). He carried it in to the kitchen table in a brown paper bag and nicked a little Easter egg from the cupboard to place on top. I ripped off the paper to find a box of 600 teabags! I suppose I do love a cup of tea with some chocolate, and it *was* better than a calf feeder.

Very organised farm husbands visit their local florist every January and hand over the credit card with a list of special dates: her birthday, their wedding anniversary, anniversary of their first date, Valentine's Day, Mother's Day if relevant, and any other dates that are special. A bouquet of flowers arrives on the appropriate day like clockwork. Organised, yes. Romantic ... hmmm.

Most gifts can be exchanged if he gets it wrong. However, a perfect farm wife commandeers a friend to do some heavy hinting and directing if she wants something special. An even better tactic is to get to know the staff at your favourite jeweller or clothing shop, and let them know your preferences so they can steer him in the right direction when he calls to buy your gift.

Of course, you could just be direct and tell him exactly what you want! He would probably be relieved.

How to ensure your other half can look after himself

Farmers aren't really recognised for their domestic skills, their ability to cook a delicious meal or choose paint colours. Might it be an advantage sometimes? You can decorate in whatever colours you choose, do your own menu planning, even stack the dishwasher in a haphazard way if you want to – knowing it will never be criticised. On the other hand, it would be handy if you could go away for a day or two and know he can look after himself.

If your man has a typical Irish mammy, he may be hopeless in terms of doing things around the house. Polishing shoes? Mammy did it on a Saturday evening for Sunday Mass. Having a cuppa? Mammy wouldn't hear of him getting his own tea. Ironing clothes? She couldn't sit by and watch him iron creases into his shirts. You have to decide if you are going to do everything for him or if you are going to make him stand on his own two feet to some extent.

My mother did everything in the house: sorting out my father's good and work clothes, polishing his shoes, ironing his clothes perfectly, leaving out his Sunday suit, cooking all meals and leaving dinners ready if she was away for the day.

Mind you, my dad coped reasonably well when Mum was away once. The house was still standing when she got back and we hadn't faded away from starvation. He's one of those farmers who doesn't spread butter on bread, he cuts slices of it. He thought the more butter he put on our sandwiches, the nicer they'd be. We couldn't eat them! He once put potatoes on to boil saying they'd be done by the time we got back from viewing a bull twenty miles away. The saucepan didn't survive.

If your mother-in-law trained your husband well, you owe her big time. As long as she didn't train him so well that he's critical of your efforts, of course!

Start the way you mean to go on. If he doesn't know how to boil an egg, use the quiet winter months to teach him some cooking and cleaning skills. Look after him well but teach him some important life skills so he won't starve if you're away. He might even cook tea for you occasionally. He'll be more inclined to help if he sees it puts you in a better mood too.

If he does help in the house, don't scare or annoy him by redoing the task or he'll never help again.

He should realise that leaving his dirty socks under the bed is almost grounds for divorce – particularly if he hasn't got to bed for the last three nights due to cows calving and they've been on his feet for the last 72 hours.

Train your sons right: your future daughters-in-law will appreciate you for it.

How to keep him well groomed

Your beloved may scarcely know where the ironing board is kept let alone decide to brandish the iron. The one huge advantage of marrying a farmer is their work clothes don't need ironing. Unlike for other business people, there are no white shirts to be starched, no suits to be brought to the dry cleaners and no shoes to be polished.

Many farmers don't worry too much about their appearance on a day-to-day basis, especially when their social life involves conversing with livestock, machinery and other farmers. Let's face it, a farmer who uses a handful of silage to wipe wet manure off his trousers isn't going to be too fussed about co-ordinating tops and bottoms first thing in the morning. They may not be the best at matching colours, choosing clothes that suit them, or even picking out clean ones, but if a farmer isn't well turned out in public, it seems to be the woman in his life (his wife or mother) who is at fault, never the farmer himself. I believe farmers should know how to find a clean pair of trousers and a shirt if going to the mart so I hold my husband wholly responsible if he appears in public with crumpled shirts or holey trousers.

Some farm wives (I'm not one of them) feel they should iron all the farm clothes. I recently heard of a farmer's wife who irons her farmer's overalls. She boils them first, as apparently if there is oil on the fabric it sticks to the iron. Who would have thought? Of course, if you see ironing as good therapy, work away, but never feel guilty for not ironing farm clothes as you'll be busy enough without doing that. The cows or other farmers won't mind the odd crease. A shake and fold should suffice. If you want to get rid of the creases, a quick tumble dry to finish the drying should work, followed by a swift iron over the shirt collars if you feel neglectful.

 If you have an Aga, place smaller items such as tea towels and pillowcases on the lids and the heat will remove the creases – if you even care about creases in tea towels of course.

For ironing bigger items, I recommend investing in a wide and long ironing board so you can iron two or three items in one go. For example, if I'm ironing a pair of jeans, I leave the iron on a trouser leg while I sort out the other item and then I iron, say, the sleeve of a shirt; when moving the shirt again, I place the iron on a different part of the jeans. The ironing is done in half the time. Don't forget to iron the bedding by placing it, folded in half, over the ironing board; by ironing other items on top of the sheet or duvet cover, it will be reasonably crease-free too so you save yourself some time.

Farm clothes are always getting snagged and ripped. If your mother-in-law still likes to do things for her "neglected" son, getting her to mend his torn clothes benefits you all.

Leaving his clothes out for him when going out for an evening can hurry him up by at least five minutes. Every minute is important when he's late already.

DOMESTIC BLISS

Even if you aren't a domestic goddess, you can still look and act the part with some confidence.

How to emphasise your domestic skills

Many farm wives in the last century were skilled in knitting, crafting and sewing. Our grandmothers made most of their own clothes, hand-sewing or with a basic machine, probably owning only two or three dresses at a time. No wonder they wore "housecoats" to protect them.

Within the ICA, there was an emphasis on learning crafts: to earn money, for recreation and to make their own clothes too. The ICA members shared their knowledge and hired teachers so each member had a chance to create beautiful crafts and to win an accolade if the craft was of high quality.[16] Clothes were expensive to buy so the ability to sew meant you could be more fashionable too. When my mother was in her early twenties, she used to buy fabric on pay day and make a new dress on her electric Singer sewing machine.

A sewing machine was a prized possession in the 1950s and 1960s. Mind you, I wonder what busy farm wives might have thought of the advice in the Singer Sewing Book by Mary Brooks Picken and published by the Singer Sewing Machine Company:

> Never approach sewing with a sigh or lackadaisical attitude. Good results are difficult when indifference predominates. Never try to sew with the sink full of dishes or bed unmade. When there are urgent housekeeping chores, do these first so that your mind is free to enjoy your sewing.
>
> When you sew, make yourself as attractive as possible. Go through a beauty ritual of orderliness. Have on a clean dress. Be sure your hands are clean, finger nails smooth — a nail file and pumice will help. Always avoid hangnails. Keep a little bag full of French chalk near your sewing machine where you can pick it up and dust your fingers at intervals. This not only absorbs the moisture on your fingers, but helps to keep your work clean. Have your hair in order, powder and lipstick put on with care. Looking attractive is a very important part of sewing, because if you are making something for yourself, you will try it on at intervals in front of your mirror, and you can hope for better results when you look your best. If you are constantly fearful that a visitor will drop in or your husband will come home and you will not look neatly put together, you will not enjoy your sewing as you should.[17]

I'm sure we all know what we'd like to do with *that* handbook. Could a farm wife rid her toughened hands of welts and broken nails before commencing her sewing, not to mention finding time to put on her lipstick?

Letters to magazines in the 1960s highlighted that these recommendations to wives to make themselves look glamorous were irrelevant for a farmer's wife. This verse from "Weary-worn" in 1966 emphasises how ridiculous it seems:

Can he just see her in buttons and bows
As she sits in her milking shed milking the cows?
Hubby's been up all night with a pig
So he won't notice her curlers or wig.[18]

Clothes and other goods are more affordable now but you can still show off your skills as all agricultural shows hold classes for various crafts. If you wish to learn, there are knitting groups and classes in almost every small town in Ireland. Alternatively, you could join the ICA or Women's Institute (WI) and choose from various activities such as cheesemaking, dressmaking, knitting, lacemaking, leather work, drama, dance, music and art. Bear in mind that once you have your membership, your man won't tolerate any holes in his clothes and will expect them to be mended and patched immediately!

 If a zip goes in a pair of your work jeans, you could use superglue to stick the two sides of the zip together rather than replacing it – as long as you can pull them up while the zip is fastened! Take them off before applying the superglue! Note: This method of repair isn't appreciated by men!

How to wear an apron and wellies with flair

Our grandmothers wore housecoats or aprons to protect their dresses but they had many more uses. Aprons were used to carry eggs in from the henhouse or apples from the orchard. They were used as oven gloves, to dust the mantelpiece if a person of importance was seen heading for the front door, and to wipe a child's tears.

Aprons seemed to go out of fashion for a while but they are making a comeback – full aprons, half aprons, frilly aprons,

aprons with pockets, patterns for making your own pinny – there's plenty of choice and yes, the right apron will make you look the part.

What about your wellies? The original "wellington boots" imitated a military boot and were made popular by the first Duke of Wellington. The first wellingtons were made of leather but by the First World War soldiers were fighting wearing boots made of rubber. Now they come in a wide array of colours and patterns.

Your style of wellies speaks volumes so choose them with care. Some people hanker after expensive branded wellies, but the cows really aren't going to mind so keep the more fashionable ones for the festivals. The problem with being a regular wellie wearer is that whenever you want to wear them to an event, they need a good scrub first. Having two pairs may be extravagant but is very handy. Colourful boots add some fun to farming and you can get bright pink and dark purple wellies in your local agricultural supply stores. Their plain colour means they aren't sufficiently fanciful to be viewed with scepticism so don't worry, once they get a bit of muck on them, you'll still be viewed as a proper farmer.

Don't get wellies that are a little tight at the top rim or you will end up with permanent "wellie indentations" on your legs if you wear them for hours each day.

HOW TO REAR YOUR FARM CHILDREN

Farm children have a very different life to other kids. Their chores extend far beyond housework and gardening. They think they are lucky to have a few days out during the summer. They're rarely bored (as they know they'll be given jobs to do if they admit such a thing) and their playground in the garden is the envy of all their friends. They can't understand how their "townie" friends manage with such small gardens.

Opening gifts on Christmas Day has to work around feeding the animals. Ride-on tractors, miniature farm machinery and Lego always features amongst gifts received.

Farming provides children with a wonderful upbringing, creating memories that will stay with them for many decades. Of course, they are living beside a busy business with huge machinery and large animals so safety has to be paramount.

How to manage your pregnancy

When you are "with child", your dearly beloved may use various farming terms to describe your pregnancy. I've heard of farm wives being asked by their partners if "their pins are going down?" as it gets close to the due date (this happens with cows before they go into labour). Listening to him debating what his birthing score might be (bovine sires have a calving score depending on how easily their offspring are born) isn't really what you want to hear either. If he starts pondering on your condition score, it really is time to shut him up.

Don't be surprised if the news of your pregnancy is initially greeted with silence as he calculates if the birth will interfere with the harvesting, calving/lambing or livestock breeding seasons. If it doesn't, he heaves a sigh of relief. Heaven forbid he might have to spend a few hours in the hospital away from the farm or he'll suggest you bring the calving camera with you so he can keep an eye from his phone!

The advantage of being self-employed means he can usually attend hospital appointments and ante-natal classes with you. He can manage the farm work around the appointments unless something crucial happens. Don't be surprised if the obstetrician, on finding out that you are both farming, asks lots of questions about the birthing of farm animals. Your farmer is in his element and you sit there wondering if they are going turn their attention to you and your unborn child.

For the birth of our second child, the waters had broken but then things came to a standstill. I was given drugs to get things going. If they had worked (they can make things happen very quickly), Brian wouldn't have been there in time as he was sorting cattle after milking before he headed over.

When he did arrive, Brian discovered that he knew our midwife and launched into a conversation about farming: if they had silage in yet, the weather, spreading fertiliser and other topics totally irrelevant to his wife and yet-to-be-born daughter, while I looked at the two of them in disbelief. "Excuse me! I'm in labour here!"

A perfect farm wife either has a home birth or lets things progress with a minimum of fuss at home so the baby is born within a few hours of reaching the hospital. A really outstanding farm wife even manages to return home within 24 hours and gets the silage contractors their tea. (For the record, I didn't do that!)

How to bring up children on the farm

Our predecessors had large families, often six to ten children, and sometimes up to eighteen! In the mid 1960s, women had an average of four babies each in Ireland, compared with two nowadays. In 1964, 2,000 babies were born to women who already had ten children. Catholic families were the most "fertile" amongst farmers and farm labourers.[19]

Work was usually segregated between boys and girls, just as it was between men and women but girls were often in the secondary role.

> There were double standards in our house. The girls polished the boys' shoes. The girls milked the cows and did a lot of the farm work. The boys were mainly prepared for the business end of it [the family had a shop and a farm]. They might have gone into Galway to pay bills or to pick up extra supplies.[20]

Girls baked and cooked, milked cows and churned butter, collected eggs and fed hens, carried water, washed dishes and clothes, and helped to look after younger siblings. Boys milked cows, fed horses, carried water and did whatever field work was going. Children were kept from school at certain times during the year such as when harvesting potatoes in the autumn. This extract emphasises the drudgery and hard work of one of the essential tasks:

Irish Independent 11 March 1958

We hated fetching water. I can remember coming in from school and seeing the row of upturned buckets on the stool inside the back door – a mute reminder that they had to be filled before tea. There was the chill of the water as it slopped over and trickled down inside your wellington, the ache in your arms despite shifting the bucket from right to left and the sinking feeling when you were told after struggling home, to "run off now, and get another".

A Co. Clare woman I interviewed still remembers that Mondays, being the clothes-washing day, demanded twenty-two buckets of water.

Men didn't really help with childcare or housework and it was a rare occurrence to see a man pushing a pram. Women reared the children, changed their nappies, got them off to school and prepared their meals. Every other woman was doing the same, regardless of their husband's occupation.

Things have changed and many fathers are more hands-on now. Non-farming dads bring their children to football training on a Saturday morning while their partners have a lie on or go shopping; you might find yourself being the only mum there. Make friends with farm wives so you can sympathise with each other. It's very easy to feel like a single parent for much of the year when married to a farmer.

On the other hand, the children can have a "go to work with Daddy" day quite frequently if safety permits. They can spend time with him on the tractor, herding, bringing in the cows to be milked or helping with feeding. He can pop in before he goes somewhere and take one of the children for half an hour. If he's heading to the barber at the same time as the kids get out of school, there's always huge excitement when Daddy collects them. When it snows, guess which kids get the most kudos when their dad arrives at the school with the tractor to bring them home.

It's lovely if children can feel they are part of the team on the farm. Having their own chores encourages a great work ethic and teaches them responsibility. However, some types of farming aren't quite so suitable for children's involvement. Some breeds of beef cattle can be wild and unruly. Others are quiet and you'll see children showing them with assured competence at the county show. Children can help on dairy and sheep farms by feeding pet lambs, giving meal to calves or bringing in the cows. Another favourite job is tending to the hens. For one of their tasks, our children scrape and put lime on the cubicles (where cows lie down and sleep) after the evening milking in February and March. They call themselves the "James Muck Cleaning Company". By owning that role, they look on it as their responsibility – and, yes, they do get paid.

 Always ensure that the playground part of the garden is secured from the farmyard; machinery is so big it can be hard to spot a small child arriving unexpectedly in the yard.

Teach your daughters to be strong-minded and independent. Only 11% of those identified as successors (to Irish farmers over 50) are female.[21] Ensure she knows that she is just as entitled to inherit the farm as her brother if she has a genuine interest in farming. Never make her feel second best.

How to create wonderful memories

If you don't want your children's memories of farming to be of long hours, hard work and little financial reward, do create some entertaining experiences for all the family. It doesn't have to involve spending lots of money or even taking time away from the farm – indeed, you can embrace what the farm has to offer.

One of my favourite childhood memories was a day trip to a spot about five miles up the hills to pick fraughans (pronounced "frockins"). We (the four children) sat on a hay bale in the transport box on a neighbour's blue Ford tractor. My recollections include itchy legs from the scratchy hay; the excitement of finding purple blue fraughans and then being disappointed as they were too bitter to eat; playing with large pieces of coal dotted around from a disused coal mine, eating ham sandwiches and queen cakes washed down with fizzy orange, before heading home, sunburnt, tired and happy. I know children can't do it now for safety reasons, but the best part was the ride in the transport box up the steep narrow road. Some things don't change, as you'll notice when attending large agricultural shows, the highlight for most children and teenagers is the trailer ride from the car park to the show.

Going to collect straw: Children love the journey on the tractor to bring straw (or hay) back to the farmyard (note that in Ireland they should be on a passenger seat with a safety belt and over the age of seven, or you could face a fine). Stopping for an ice cream on the way home is always a highlight.

Silage: Silage time makes for great memories: travelling with one of the contractors for a while, staying up late (as they won't fall asleep anyway with the noise of the trundling tractors and trailers) and the picnics to the field.

Picnics: If their dad is going to be late home for dinner during the summer, pack it all up and bring dinner to the field so you can eat together. You can't be a farm kid and not have memories of grass or corn stubble scratching your legs while eating a farm picnic.

Picking conkers: Horse chestnuts aren't edible but make ideal mini silage bales or cattle feed for a young boy or girl who loves playing with their toy machinery. Collecting full buckets of conkers is a nice way to spend an hour or two, especially if you bring a little picnic too. If you dry them out in a low oven they will last for years! Yes, you will be vacuuming them up occasionally!

Snowed in: The benefit of living in an isolated spot is that when it snows, you're cut off from all other civilisation. You mightn't be so keen but the children will be delighted. Days off school, sliding down a hill on a homemade toboggan made from an old sheet of galvanised roofing, building snowmen and being collected from school on the tractor all make farm living special for kids.

Newborns: While the novelty of newborns wears off after a while, there's always huge excitement when the first calf, lamb, cria, goat kid or litter of piglets of the year are born, especially if they can help to feed them. They like to name them and you're expected to remember all the names too.

Foraging: Children love picking blackberries – until, that is, they have been picking for ages and can still see the bottom of the bucket. To help them along (and stop the whinging before it starts), give them small sandcastle buckets and tip some of your pickings into theirs. Picking field mushrooms is much easier as the buckets fill quickly. Freshly picked mushrooms for breakfast or supper are delicious.

Baking: During my childhood, Saturday was always the main baking day, often in preparation for visitors on Sunday. The smells of baking in the kitchen, the noise of rugby commentary from the living room and the taste of hot queen cakes just out of the oven are some of my favourite childhood recollections. Whatever day of the week you decide to bake, get the children involved. They love making shapes with bits of pastry and surprising their dad with their cakes.

Competitions: Agricultural shows always have competitions for children to enter their drawings, handwriting examples, knitting, crafts, pony riding skills or baking. Create memories by entering their efforts in a couple of classes. It adds much more interest to the show when they are wondering if they've won and perhaps walking away with a prize.

How to tell farm children about sex

Living on a farm means children will see baby animals being created. This provides them with an interesting introduction to sex education and can lead to amusing questions and comments.

Answer their questions truthfully with information appropriate to their age. On seeing rams and ewes getting down to business, an eight-year-old asked what the ram was doing. On hearing they were making baby lambs, she replied "Mummy, thank goodness Daddy didn't have to jump on your back for you to have us."

When our son was aged five years, whenever he saw the AI technician driving up the yard, he used to tell his little sister, using a very self-important and knowledgeable tone of voice, that "he has gone up to put a seed into the cow which will grow into a calf". I often wondered if he was visualising an apple seed; I might leave it a few years yet before asking him.

Make sure the context is correct before you go into too much detail.

How to encourage children to farm

Succession is a really important topic, yet people don't tend to talk about it. Most farmers really want to see the family farming tradition continued with one of their children taking over the farm. There's a Sod's Law situation with this, as if there are six children in the family, chances are they'll either all want to farm or none of them will.

Some argue farming is either in a person's blood or it isn't. If a person is forced into it, out of guilt, loyalty or lack of choices, their heart isn't going to be in it. Ultimately, then, the farm will go downhill as a result.

It is usually males who inherit, partly because farming is seen as a "male" occupation and perhaps to keep the family name with the land. Shortall states this patrilineal line of inheritance reinforces the image of farms being male-owned with women as assistants.[22] In the past, women inherited only if they were the only daughter, and even then they weren't necessarily classed as farmers if they were married. In the 1901 census, Kate Carr and her husband were both described as farmers. However, in 1911, she was placed in the "Unoccupied" category. Although she or her husband initially wrote she was a farmer, someone, presumably the census enumerator, crossed through this and with the stroke of a pen demoted her status.[23] In 1961, 3.9% of brides declared themselves to be farmers, although the real figure may have been higher as one-third of all brides didn't declare an occupation. By 1990, the figure had reduced, with 0.7% of the total 17,838 Irish brides being farmers in their own right (125 women).[24]

Today, 12% of Ireland's registered farmers are female, yet the number of women farming is much higher. Between women working alongside the herd owner and some women farming full-time while husbands (the registered farmers) work elsewhere, the "hidden" female farmers are more common than you might think.

Some parents try to discourage daughters from farming, seeing it as too difficult or not a suitable career for women. Having spoken to women who are working as sheep, suckler, tillage and dairy farmers, all feel they are well able for it. There are areas where women have to be careful; for example, lambing sheep while pregnant can be dangerous for the unborn child. However, it's all about making enough income to delegate occasionally, just as men do.

There are many reasons why children might decide they don't want to farm. These include seeing parents working constantly, all work and no play, negativity in farming, few holidays and stressing children out when they are helping. Maybe they just don't like working with animals or they've had enough of manure. Perhaps they want to travel the world and get a "good job". Sometimes the world of employment isn't what it seems though; at least in farming your targets are self-inflicted! Many adults admit they didn't want to farm when in their late teens and early twenties but see it as a wonderful career once in their thirties.

A farm is a business as well as being a physical entity that holds so much attachment. Succession advisers believe not talking about the future of the farm threatens its future viability. If children want to farm, help them to plan their education, see if travelling to farms abroad would be advantageous and work out how the farm will provide two incomes if that is required. It's a good idea to get a facilitator to ensure all of the children are happy so no one feels short-changed.

Like the birds, set them free. They might return.

Give them a childhood to enjoy. Celebrate the successes, create wonderful memories and let them see what a wonderful life farming can be.

How to share childcare

This is a challenge for many farming families if one person farms full-time and the other is employed elsewhere. Some couples even manage two full-time jobs with part-time farming. If children are in school, so much has to be organised: dropping to the school bus, collecting them, homework, bringing them to activities, and making sure they are playing safely. Some opt to send their children to an after-school club, childminder or crèche, but if it is a busy time of year on the farm and you are delayed at work, it's stressful rushing to collect them.

Some men prefer their wife to help out on the farm and look after the children. They resist their plans to return to work after maternity leave or when the children start school. It really is all down to personal preference and monetary need. For some people, being a full-time mum on the farm is just too claustrophobic. They want the intellectual challenge of work, the company of adults and, yes, the income is nice too.

There's no doubt about it, being employed while farming presents challenges when you have children. Much depends on the ability to be flexible. There's no right or wrong solution as every situation is different. It helps hugely if you have someone, such as a grandparent, who can collect the children if both of you are delayed or who can look after a sick child on occasion.

HEALTH AND SAFETY

Farming is one of the most dangerous occupations worldwide, coming second only to mining. Working with big animals and large machinery, sometimes under pressure of time, means farm accidents happen all too often. Farmers seem to think they are invincible until it happens to them. While accidents also happened in the past, it was rare that farmers worked on their own so there was someone there to raise the alarm. Many now work in isolation so if something happens it could be hours before they are discovered.

We do have more safety measures in place now – for example, cattle chutes (crushes) and calving gates to restrain bovines. I have to admit I shudder when I read James Herriot's tales of farmers catching three-year-old bullocks and holding on by the horns. However, animals are unpredictable and when they are large a human body isn't able to put up that much resistance.

Safety isn't just about physical health either. A bad year in farming can take its toll on mental and emotional health too.

This section is about how you can aim to get a good balance between farm work and time off.

How to get a farmer to take a holiday

You may read this heading and think to yourself "but we go on holidays every year". If that's the case, well done! Yes, many larger operators have hired labour or regular relief milkers so they can get away. There's an increase in farm partnerships too so they can take it in turns to hold the fort.

There are also lots of farmers who resist the notion of a holiday because they love what they do. They believe that no one else can look after their animals as well as they can. Many are total workaholics and have the attitude "better to wear out than rust out"! Dairy farmers can be the worst, between the cost of a relief milker and thinking about their grass management, they can have every argument under the sun not to go away while the cows are milking.

Employed people can take a few days off work and stay at home to relax. They can catch up on decorating tasks, meet friends, have visitors to stay, read books and chill out. It's next to impossible for a farmer to stay at home and not work. Sometimes you do just need to book that flight, arrange a hotel or go camping for a few days. Even a "working holiday" of visiting farms abroad is worth doing: a change is as good as a rest after all.

Some farm couples go on separate holidays at different times of the year. They can take it in turns to relax and enjoy time away knowing the farm is in safe hands. He might go on a farm-themed holiday while she visits friends or heads to the sun with the girls. There's no need for arguments about stopping off at a mart while sight-seeing!

Some get their part-time farmhand to cover for the week when they are away. Others go for a week in January when the farm is at its quietest and recharge their batteries before the calving/lambing/sowing starts. Mind you, it can happen that he pines for his cows when separated from them! I'd recommend going to a warmer climate as the change in temperature helps him to "get away from it all" and it takes much less time to get into the "holiday zone".

Alternatively, go for quick hotel breaks of 30 hours! Get the work done early in the morning and leave around midday, returning at 6pm the next day to catch up on all the necessary jobs for that day. If you're a dairy farmer, the cows won't begrudge being milked by the relief milker for two milkings.

If you haven't married him yet, consider the wedding date carefully if you want to be able to celebrate your anniversaries with a holiday or a night out. There won't be any chance of getting away for anniversary celebrations if you get married during the calving/lambing, the sowing or the harvest. He may have plenty of help on the farm now which enables him to get away for the honeymoon, but that could change in future years!

How to cope with stress

There's no doubt about it, farming is a stressful occupation. Men in general can find it difficult to talk about their feelings and their worries, but multiply that many times for farmers. There's a feeling of responsibility towards parents for inheriting the farm, the wish to hand it on to the next generation, and the stress of coping with what life throws at him and you.

Stresses include:

- Meeting repayments to the bank.
- Reduced income due to lowering prices.
- An accident on the farm.
- Machinery breakdowns which are expensive to repair.
- Sick or dying animals.
- Atrocious weather, especially during the summer.
- Feeling under pressure to be successful.

One way to reduce stress is to try and prevent the causes. We can't do much about world market prices or the weather, but financial planning, consultations with your vet or agricultural adviser and having a business plan can help prepare for the worst eventualities.

Concentrate on what you can control inside the farm gate before worrying about outside factors. World trade prices are taken into account in business planning and loan repayments, but you can't do much about it this week. Be proactive, not reactive. If your income takes a dip and it's difficult to make repayments to the bank, tell your bank manager but don't let them add to the pressure. You do own a valuable asset after all. I remember one farmer saying "pressure is only for tyres and blow-up dolls". If nothing else, remembering that line will make you smile when you're looking at your bank statement.

Some farmers get stressed over the same things every year, things that they can't do anything about – it's a habit. They become so fraught and hormonal, it's like a male version of PMS but in his case it is Pre Silage Stress, Pre TB Test Tension, Pre Factory Trauma, Pre Mart Stress, Pre Harvest Tension and Pre Lambing Anxiety. Even though he knows there's nothing he can do about the results of the annual tuberculosis test, those three days of waiting are filled with anxiety. Silage contractors do the majority of the work but he won't be able to sit still between checking the weather forecast, wondering when to tell them to come, working out how long it will take them to finish the farmer before him, debating if he is cutting too soon, and wondering if he waits will he be caught by rain?

Another concern is the "right time" to sell animals at the mart or to the factory. Should he sell animals this week as they've been going up in price? What if he sells and they go up more? What if he doesn't sell this week and the price goes down? You have to listen to all this by the way, while staying sane and making soothing noises. He needs to hear a calm and rational voice telling him to make a decision and live with it.

Stressed farmers say things they don't really mean. There's no point getting upset about it. You just have to remember that he loves you and at that moment, your presence is really getting on his nerves because the whole world is irritating him – the dog, the grass, the cows, the rain, the sunshine and, yes, you too.

We were scanning cows one day to check pregnancies and I'd totally forgotten about it. I was living "in the moment" sorting school lunches and finding missing socks. "You're as useful as sunglasses in fog" was what I heard as he stomped back up the yard disappearing into the grey mist. "Hmmm, hormonal," I thought as I got the kids off to school. He was anxious because a favourite (and pregnant) cow had shown signs of being on heat the day before which meant she had lost the calf. Hence, he was wondering if there were any other nasty surprises lurking.

While you have to search for the compliments, bad language can come thick and fast on a farm. Believe the flattering remarks but never consider he means what he says when it comes to insults. You have to believe you are good at what you do, otherwise a statement such as "feckin eejit" when you leave a gate open might get you down, so take them with a very large pinch of salt. Silence is sometimes the best answer initially but if it goes on for too long, give as good as you get.

 Remember HALT: the symptoms of stress arise when he is Hungry, Angry, Lonely or Tired. Getting food, a chance to relax after dinner, a good night's sleep and talking it over can make problems diminish overnight. It's true, laughter is the best medicine, so getting out for an evening and having a laugh is as good as a tonic. If he is depressed during the day but shows signs of being in a happier mood in the evenings, it's probably because the day is nearly over and he doesn't have to deal with stuff. That's when professional help like counselling is useful.

And if you have one of those farmers who take it all in their stride, count your blessings. I know I do. After all, I wouldn't be able to write this book otherwise, would I?

How to keep your family safe

Look at the farmyard with fresh eyes on a regular basis so you can see the dangers and either remove them or make them safe. It's easy to think that something you do every day is perfectly safe. Everyday occurrences can present unexpected dangers. Freshly calved cows can be dangerous as they are instantly protective of their newborns. Never tag a calf when the mother is in the same pen: one head-butt from her could finish you off.

The obvious danger on livestock farms are male animals with their surging testosterone. Don't turn your back on a ram, and be very careful with bulls. More farmers are doing bull beef now so having 50–100 yearling bulls in sheds is becoming more commonplace. If they are in a field and you have the job of herding (checking) them occasionally, look at them from over the ditch. When moving or loading them, your working dog is worth his weight in gold.

Many years ago, when doing the annual tuberculosis test, one bull was in the yard after being tested and the other bull broke through to him. They started fighting immediately. The stronger one pushed the other back against a gate, the gate gave way and they both fell into the dungstead (dung pit) which was up to ten feet deep in places. We watched as they sank below the top of the dung only to emerge again and again with loud bellows as they continued to fight each other for hours. Nothing could be done without risking our own lives. Eventually, exhausted and shivering, they stood in the yard, having made their way out, too tired to fight anymore.

Don't let kids ride in a trailer or in an open doorway of a tractor. We all did it when we were young though. When I was about eight, I was sitting happily in a trailer going over to the out-farm. The tractor was going down a hill and I was being jostled around a bit as it went faster. There were a number of big bumps and then little reverberating ones until the trailer stopped. I scrambled to my knees and saw the tractor driving away. "Tommeeeeee!" I shrieked. I'm sure he couldn't have heard me but he turned around and did a huge double-take to see the trailer almost in the ditch and my worried face peeping out over the frontboard. It was as simple as the pin falling out of the tow bar. At least the trailer didn't try to overtake the tractor I guess!

Don't assume children know what to do when helping so take the time to explain things to them. Sometimes they will do things that you never imagined might happen. You have to be thinking a couple of steps ahead all the time.

I'm sure my dad thought I'd never be so silly as to climb down the front of a trailer of straw bales. I was about ten when helping him to load bales onto a borrowed trailer. We had secured the ropes and just as I was about to climb down, two men came into the field and my father ambled over to say hello. As it is with farmers, a quick hello turns into an in-depth conversation about the weather, the quality of the straw and who hasn't got theirs baled yet. I needed his help to point out the toeholds amongst the bales, but getting bored I decided to climb down on my own. Peering down the back of the load, it looked like we had built it much more steeply than the last time and I couldn't see any little ledges to use as footholds on the way down, and it was a *long* way down.

I walked to the front and looked down. The front bales were stacked just as steeply but this trailer had a high front board on it. I knew it was the same height as the first three rows of bales. Surely I would be able to get my toes in over the board to get a grip and from there I could jump down onto the drawbar and hop down. Easy-peasy. The only question was what could I hold onto as my feet searched for the ledge. The twines of course, I could get my fingers in behind the twines at the end of the bales and I'd be fine.

I got down on my knees and grabbed a twine with one hand. There was a rush of air and a loud thud. I opened my eyes to see three worried faces looking down at me.

The bales at the front were packed tighter than anywhere else on the trailer. It was a vertical slide. I had forgotten the row of bales over the front board jutted out slightly so there was no way to secure a toehold even if I had managed to hold onto twines. There was very little space between tractor and trailer in which to jump and not hit anything. If my head had hit the drawbar linking the two machines, it probably would have been the end of me. Luckily, I only ended up with a sore leg and a bruised ego.

Ensure that you have emergency numbers to hand: the local fire station, hospital, doctor, and not forgetting your vet. Make sure your children know how to phone these too, as soon as they are old enough.

Keep your first-aid kit stocked.

When working with animals, spend time planning and preparing. Setting up more gates when working with livestock can make a job easier and safer.

Don't get frazzled!

How to stay healthy

Apparently farmers are seven times more likely to die from a cardiovascular disease than people in other occupations, according to research by the Irish Heart Foundation. [25] The study focused on farmers attending the mart. Of course, this could be interpreted as seasoned mart attendees not being as fit as other farmers. However, it is true that farmers aren't as physically active as their predecessors; for a start, they drive around on quads instead of walking. Their machinery is doing the work instead of the farmer having to fork hay or pitch bales. Rather than walking, cycling or riding a horse to the out-farm, they are driving the tractor or jeep.

If you are working off farm, your nearest and dearest might be getting a huge dinner and dessert from his mammy and having another dinner with you in the evening. Think of all those extra calories and fats and sugars!

Keep an eye on those double desserts as well as the dinners. You don't want to receive his life assurance yet. Combine a good walk through the fields with getting fresh air and enjoying the peace and quiet. And don't forget to treat it as a date.

HOW TO STAY MARRIED

No one gets married with plans to divorce, and with their immense affection for the land, farmers in particular want their relationships to last and their children to inherit. Prenuptial agreements are all very well, but couples with happy marriages have farm businesses that thrive.[26]

How to recognise a compliment

Farmers don't tend to be big talkers and certainly don't offer tributes or praise very often. Indeed, unless you know how to recognise a farmer's compliment, you may miss it completely.

Examples of compliments:

- "If you were a beef heifer, I'd be doing well." – He doesn't mind that you've put on a bit of weight.
- "That cake is nearly as good as my mother's." – High praise indeed.
- "The bit of weight suits you." – Hmmm, is it said with a sarcastic tone?

- "You can run faster than I thought." – Goodness, that's a good tribute especially if you were running after cattle or sheep.

- "That was a grand dinner." – Getting such flattery on your cooking means you should enter that dish in every suitable competition going.

- "You're a hardy woman." – This doesn't necessarily mean that you are physically strong but that you are astute, work smart as well as hard and have a good business head.

- "You're some tulip." – Hmm, not really a flattering remark but a less harsh way of saying you're a feckin' eejit.

Just assume everything he says about you is a compliment. Even if it includes the word "feckin", it's likely his way of being endearing.

How to get on well with your mother-in-law

The extended family might be working in the business, depending on its size. If that's the case, family members of various generations live close together and many work long hours on the farm. The older couple usually like to stay living on the farm even if retired, so you are probably living within shouting distance of their house. It might feel a tad suffocating and claustrophobic at times.

Mothers-in-law tend to have a bad reputation, commonly cast in films and soap operas as being interfering, self-righteous, jealous and desperate to keep the power they hold within the farm structure and the community. Is that accurate? Is she really a villain or is she misunderstood?

Different types of mothers-in-law (on a sliding scale)

- She is grateful someone married her son as she had given up on him. She might think you are mad to have married him so will welcome you with open arms.

- She is over the moon to have a daughter-in-law (particularly if she has all boys) and is excited about the prospect of grandchildren.

- She isn't happy with anything you do and lets everyone know.

- She wants to maintain the ownership (and keep the income) of the farm, and requires her son to work for a pittance. She expects you to work off farm and yet help out in your "spare time". She might even call you a gold-digger if she believes (or wants to believe) you are interested only in the value of the farm.

- She seems determined to set her children against each other and views any input from you as unwelcome interference.

Ironically, it seems the women who experienced a tough time from their mother-in-law make their daughters-in-law suffer. As the expression goes, it is a case of "poacher turned gamekeeper".

Some farmers' wives are great friends with their mother-in-law, even if they share the same house. This seems to work best if the younger woman stays working and her mother-in-law looks after the children and the house. Some women believe it works because they slotted into a "daughter" role rather than trying to challenge anything in the household. Others say they get on great with their mother-in-law but there is an inherent tension between them. The older woman feels "I made him, you owe me" while the daughter-in-law reacts with "He picked me, I'm his first priority now".

Realistically, for most women, the experience of sharing a kitchen let alone a house with another woman who is not a blood relative or a partner is going to have its moments. As Lisdoonvarna matchmaker Willie Daly says, "More than one woman in a kitchen is a recipe for disaster".[27] It's nobody's fault: it's not possible to get on all the time. Everyone has their own habits which eventually drive the other person mad. It may be how the table is set or if one person leaves the toaster out on the worktop. Do you remember the days of sharing a kitchen with flatmates and being irritated because they didn't wash up or because someone ate something of yours? Those little things can start to grate on your nerves.

Ireland's Taoiseach during the 1930s, Eamonn de Valera, noticed the need for a separate house for the parents. There was widespread concern about farmers' sons inheriting farms so late in life and either remaining bachelors or being elderly when they eventually married. De Valera wanted the government to fund the building of cottages where the parents could live, while the younger couples lived in the farmhouses and were guaranteed to inherit the farm within ten years.

Nenagh Guardian 11 September 1937
... a cottier's house on every small farm, which would enable the eldest boy to get married without having to wait for years until the farm came into his possession through the death of his parents.

It was believed that as inheritance was delayed, the farmers were often too set in their ways to marry or gave in when mothers resisted the idea of a daughter-in-law. The dower house scheme didn't happen due to lack of funding and was proposed again in the 1950s. Again, it was a futile exercise.

Two generations sharing a house was common until the 1970s, but it is now rare in Ireland. If your in-laws are moving to another house, perhaps a new bungalow on the farm, and you are going to live in the farmhouse, set some boundaries from the outset. I recall hearing of a newlywed bride who woke to find her mother-in-law had popped into her bedroom. Talk about a step too far! Calling in for a cup of tea without knocking might be fine but it means it is hard to achieve privacy. The last thing you want is a "knowledgeable" mother-in-law dropping in when the dinner is burning or one of your children is having a tantrum on the kitchen floor.

If you are living in the original farmhouse, you might find she resents changes to the decor. That orange and brown swirly "perfectly good carpet" chosen with love and care in the 1970s might have retro appeal but it isn't necessarily the look you want. You have to choose between making changes little and often or getting them done in one fell swoop.

Farming parents often worry their daughter-in-law might divorce their son, resulting in half the farm being sold to finance the settlement. Apart from the sale affecting the future profitability of the business, there is the dread of losing land that has been in the family for generations. This fear can influence their decision to delay the transfer. In many ways, history is repeating itself, similar to Ireland of the 1950s when fathers held onto land until they died. Sons didn't inherit until middle-aged or elderly. A delay in inheriting the farm can lead to problems since the young couple can't get loans to improve or extend the farm as it isn't in their name. The daughter-in-law might be left out of farming decisions and may feel powerless and frustrated. As a result, she doesn't get involved which can be viewed as disinterest.

Remember that you have your own future to think of too. God forbid, but if anything happened to your husband and the farm is not in his name, you have very little security – maybe not even the house you live in. Being young, newly married and still financially independent is one thing, but it would be a very different situation if you have young children, don't have an off-farm income and little involvement in the farm business.

For all concerned, the future of the farm business and how it will be handled is an important topic that should be sorted with some conversation around the table, perhaps with the help of a facilitator.

Take a moment to try to understand your mother-in-law (if that's not too big an ask!).

' Be grateful that mothers-in-law are less powerful now. They used to try to maintain their role of queen bee in the hive, with access to inside knowledge on everything in the farm and parish. Whereas they once stayed living in the family home, perched on their armchair thrones in the corner of the kitchen, they now tend to live in new bungalows, situated a short distance away from the farm.

' Consider your mother-in-law to be a useful ally rather than an adversary. Ask her for advice and tips and she might enjoy sharing her knowledge with you. She might even share some baking tips.

' Don't put your spouse in the middle if you can help it.

' When building a new home, ensure each house has some privacy. Just because you are in-laws, it doesn't mean that you have lots of things in common. Life would be great if you did but you're still going to need your own space.

' Set boundaries if necessary.

' Unless she actually tells you you're a gold-digger, she probably means well by her "helpful comments" – in her own way. As a result of being attached to the farm, she may be experiencing withdrawal symptoms and doesn't want to let go her ties to it. She might also want to keep her son holding onto her apron strings.

' Don't feel you have to be a carbon copy of your mother-in-law. Find your own place on the farm by taking on a role you enjoy.

' A caring mother-in-law makes a wonderful grandmother and they are usually delighted to look after the children after school or when you want a few hours off to go shopping. Work with her, appreciate her for what she does and reward her for her help.

' Remember you might be a mother-in-law some day!

' If she is difficult, remember that the more power you give her, the more formidable she becomes. Take inspiration from dairy cows. Watch them as they walk in to be milked, particularly if strutting along a road. They aren't bothered by the waiting cars. The dog might nip at their heels and they'll quicken their step for a moment but not before kicking out. Don't let other people antagonise you. The cows saunter with confidence looking relaxed and graceful. They are strong and stoical. They know what they have to do and are happy to do it but they won't be pressurised if they can help it. Follow their lead, act confidently and you'll be treated with respect.

How to plan for success and celebrate it when it comes

A farm is a living and breathing business. It can be both interesting and exciting to be involved in plans for it. Setting goals and planning strategies together are part of effective team-building but don't forget to reward yourselves with some team-bonding afterwards. Discussing what bulls to use on cows is much more interesting when you know exactly how you want to improve the herd. Going shopping for a new ram might not match shoe-shopping, but it definitely raises the game if you're hoping for award-winning sheep in the future. Being a perfect farm wife doesn't just involve knowing the names of the fields; it is also about planning goals and realising the dreams of the farm business and, yes, it is often the wife who gives the farmer the confidence to go for it.

What are the best days in farming? When the harvest is in and it's a good crop. When he returns from the mart with an empty trailer happy with the price for the stock. When the sun is shining, the grass is growing and the cows are chewing their cud contentedly. When your prize heifer wins a ribbon at an agricultural show. When you stand in one of your fields and look at the view, feeling you're on top of the world.

Farming tends to be rush, rush, rush and once one task is completed, it is onto the next project. Farmers don't often stop to mark the wins. If there is something to celebrate, big or small, go out for a meal or bake a special cake. It helps the children to see that farming isn't all about hard work too. Even a good meal with a nice bottle of wine helps you to remember the good times and strive for more success.

How to avoid a divorce

Divorce in farm families can have deeper consequences than most other situations because of the familial tie to the land. It doesn't always follow that the non-farming spouse gets half the farm, but part of it might have to be sold to finance the settlement. This can cause huge upset and consternation and is one of the reasons why girlfriends are sometimes treated with so much suspicion (and described as gold-diggers) by prospective in-laws.

It's very easy to romanticise marriage and see living on a farm as the "good life", the rural idyll where the sun is always shining and you work as a team with never a cross word between you. Comparing it to a 40-hour working week doesn't help either as you'll constantly be annoyed when he doesn't arrive in at a decent time in the evenings. If you like being organised, it takes time to acclimatise to the fact it's difficult to plan the simplest things, like having a family day off together. At least when you don't get to take too many days off, you appreciate them all the more!

 If you both hate doing a particular job and it is causing arguments, hire someone to do it. If paperwork is a problem, take on a bookkeeper and just throw everything into a shoebox. It makes it much easier than arguing about mislaid paperwork. Delegating and outsourcing are a lot cheaper than a divorce.

Use sorting the livestock as a means to get frustration out of your system. You know you both forget about the angst afterwards and put it all down to his poor communication skills. Don't use it as an excuse to get started and bring up every other reason he drives you mad.

Start the way you mean to go on. If seeing his dirty clothes on the floor fills you with annoyance in the early days of marriage, you are going to be fit to explode by the time you've had two children. Get him to drop them into "his" laundry basket from day one. If he asks "What's for dinner?" minutes after you've both finished a farm task, pass him the potato peeler. It's up to you if you want to use a stabbing motion when handing it over.

Ensure there's equality with finance. If you plan to give up off-farm work to care for the children and you're going to be working on the farm, have equal access to the cheque book.

Communication is key, sharing a dream and working towards it, understanding disappointment when things don't work out, having a laugh, taking time out. And remember what I said about those compliments? Keep an eye out for them! It's good to feel appreciated.

How to find the silver lining

Some people see farmers as pessimistic, that they are always complaining, never pleased when things go right or if the weather is good. There are so many things to deal with between Mother Nature, market prices of outputs and inputs, grass growth, crop yield, illness and death. Some believe bad events happen in threes so if they've had bad luck twice, they are almost waiting for the next misfortune. But are they as miserable as they seem?

Farmers would never stay in the business if they were negative all the time. If things are going well, they almost feel too superstitious to admit to good fortune, believing the next thing will go wrong if they tempt fate, using expressions such as "not bad" rather than "good", or "ticking along" instead of "flying it". Indeed, if a farmer, when asked "How are things?" replies with a really positive response such as "Great" or "Fantastic" he will be viewed with suspicion of telling lies.

If negative things do happen, if they are having a tough year, they try to see the silver lining. If an animal has died, farmers tend to say "as long as it's all in the yard", or "as long as it's not in the house", meaning if no one in the family is ill, it will all be okay. And if it is a poor year financially, there will be less money going to the Revenue!

If farmers weren't so optimistic, they might be shrewder businesspeople. Indeed, less optimism might result in there being no fat cattle or sheep in the country some years. If farmers get a poor price for their cattle in the factory, they still go back to the mart to buy young stock in the expectation that prices will be better the following year. They enjoy what they do and are always hopeful for better prices.

Although you (unlike some of the cows) are too realistic to think that the grass might be greener on the other side, you always have a "glass half full" attitude. Otherwise, you'll be sobbing all the way to the bank on a regular basis.

There will be days when it is hard to see the positives. As a farm wife, if things are getting to him, it's your role to point them out if he can't see them. Even things like comparing a long commute stuck in traffic to his stroll across the fields are worth seeing as advantageous. If that only serves to irritate, then you both need some TLC: Tea, Love and Chocolate.

How to conceal your mood

Family farming means you are working with your nearest and dearest but that doesn't mean they won't drive you mad at times. Even a perfect farm wife is allowed to be slightly grumpy and hormonal occasionally. However, you can disguise it by using words opposite to what you mean. The trick is using an appropriate tone of voice so others don't suspect your sarcasm.

🍵 "Fine." – Used when you're feeling grumpy and your husband has just asked how you are. This signals that he should not say "You're not fine, what's wrong?", or "What's up with you then?", which only serve to infuriate you more.

🍵 "That's nice." – Sod off with your boasting and bragging about your first prize in the show.

🍵 "You're welcome." – If through gritted teeth, this means someone has one up on you and you're not going to let them know.

🍵 "Oh, how lovely!" – Please don't tell me about your holiday to the Caribbean as I haven't even got to Kerry for the last five years.

🍵 "Do call again, anytime!" – Oh, please don't, and if I see you coming, I'll be heading out to bring in the cows.

🍵 "Whatever." – I really don't care what you do, I'm busy and don't have time for this bellyaching about something inconsequential.

How to have a social life

Sometimes it can feel that the farm is work, work, work and even those tractor dates can get a bit tedious after a while, especially if the conversation revolves around crops or the engine size of the new tractor. Sometimes, the only time you have a "best hair day", there's only the livestock to appreciate it as your partner is too preoccupied to notice.

It *is* possible to get out there and have a social life. If his idea of socialising includes attending farm meetings where they moan about beef prices; going to a vintage tractor club, which means you are a passenger when he's tootling along on his vintage runs, or taking part in stock judging when they compare udders amongst other things, you might decide to take up some hobbies of your own.

Living on a farm means it can be a downward slippery slope to becoming a hermit. If you want to get to know people in the area, join a book club, an ICA/WI group or the local sports club. Some book clubs chat about the book for five minutes and then move to more important matters like news and gossip; others stick rigidly to the book, so know what you want before you join up!

In the past, some farm women had a limited social life. The only outing for many was their monthly ICA meeting. Men and women didn't even go to the pub together: women weren't allowed into pubs until the late 1960s and were even fined if they were brave enough to enter the doors. Eventually "snugs" were built – a little room off the main bar, where women could sit and chat within the confined space. Before that, wives finished their weekly shopping and waited in the car or trap until their husbands finished drinking in the pub.

My paternal grandmother rarely went to town shopping. Her husband drove in weekly, left the shopping list in the grocery store and called to see his brother for a while, returning to collect the groceries later. It sounds like supermarket shopping was much more civilised then! She didn't join the ICA but attended the local Mothers' Union meeting once a month. I had presumed that surely the weekly church service would provide her with a couple of hours out but no, cooking the dinner for her large family meant she stayed at home as the range had to be kept hot. However, they received lots of visitors. Her husband's brother came every weekend, and relatives and neighbours called up every Sunday afternoon. She used to make eight apple tarts every Saturday and not a crumb would be left on the Sunday evening.

Two Co. Clare women recalled how their parents either hosted or visited a ceili in a neighbour's house almost every night of the week. Their house was filled with music and dancing every Wednesday evening and they took it in their turn to visit others. It sounds like a quiet night in was very rare indeed.

Years ago, neighbours visited each other regularly too. Once the work was done, they'd call to each other to tell stories and play cards, often playing poker for matches. The lane running at the back of our farm is now quiet as the few houses dotted along it are empty and derelict but it once served as a shortcut from the school and church to a townland. Schoolchildren and Mass-goers trooped along it as did people visiting neighbours at night, using the light of the moon to see their way.

If you're now thinking the social life half a century ago sounded better than yours, you need to start getting out there.

When going out, check the contents of your handbag before you open it in front of other people. Most women have handbags containing a medley of accessories. These probably include a packet of tissues, make-up, a small mirror, a hairbrush, business cards, their mobile phone and a purse. Your handbag might be more like an industrial satchel or toolbag. Add to those items a pair of pliers, a few blue cards (animal passports), a cheque book with dubious-looking stains, invoices to be paid, scraps of paper with notes of what the farmer wants from town, a few nuts and bolts, paracetamol and maybe a thermometer for animals (not to be confused and used on humans!).

FARM WIFE QUIZ (1)

1. You're planning a holiday. Do you:
   (a) Arrange for cover for the farm and book a "farm tour" holiday abroad for the two of you
   (b) Arrange a week's holiday for the slackest time of the year
   (c) Decide to head off to the sun with a few friends?

2. It's getting close to silage time and he's wondering when to tell the contractors to cut the grass. Do you:
   (a) Check out every possible weather forecast and bring the samples of grass to be tested for nitrogen, doing a grocery shop on the way
   (b) Prepare for the pre-silage tension by buying lots of chocolate as you know his PST will last until all silage is in the pit and covered
   (c) Think about visiting the seaside for a couple of days with the children?

3. The farmer knocks on the kitchen window, asks if you are busy and says he wants some help for five minutes. Do you:
   (a) Sigh inwardly, turn down the oven so the dinner doesn't burn and pull on your wellies and coat knowing you will be outside for at least an hour
   (b) Say "no problem" and run out in your crocs, expecting it to take five minutes
   (c) Glower at him and say you're busy cooking dinner?

4. His extended family are doing "Secret Santa" this year and you've drawn your mother-in-law's name out of the hat. Do you buy her:
   (a) Her favourite perfume because you know she will love it
   (b) An airplane ticket to go and see relatives abroad for a few weeks
   (c) A scarf, since someone told you they weren't the safest clothing for farms?

5. Your farmer falls asleep in an armchair when visiting your relatives. Do you:
   (a) Put a cushion under his head so he won't wake up with a sore neck, wishing you could join him
   (b) Cringe and hope he doesn't snore too loudly, saying you'll wake him in fifteen minutes
   (c) Kick his foot to wake him and hope nobody notices?

6. You go into labour with your second child. Do you:
   (a) Decide to finish spreading the fertiliser first just in case you're not home again for a few days
   (b) Pack your bag for the hospital while timing contractions, checking that you've left him with written instructions for defrosting all the meals you've left in the freezer
   (c) Ring the hospital to tell them you're leaving immediately while your husband carries your huge suitcase to the car? If having a baby means you can get meals in bed for a week, you're going to enjoy every minute.

7. It's your wedding anniversary and he suggests you accompany him to sell lambs, stopping for a quick pub lunch on the way home. Do you:
   (a) Say no problem, you were going to go with him anyway. Lunch out and his undivided attention for an hour, what a wonderful way to spend your anniversary
   (b) Agree but get him to promise to a meal out on Saturday night
   (c) Refuse. How dare he think he can palm you off with a quick lunch in a pub?

8. He agrees to a special night out. Do you:
   (a) Prepare for something to go wrong and have a backup plan
   (b) Nag him to make sure nothing goes wrong
   (c) Go shopping for new clothes and go and get your hair done?

How did you do?

Mostly A's – you're a born farmer / farmer's wife and embrace everything about the farming lifestyle.

Mostly B's – you're well on the way to becoming a perfect farm wife. Keep it up.

Mostly C's – ahem, maybe try a little harder with the next section.

PART THREE

THE FARM

Proverbs:

A wet and windy May fills the haggard with corn and hay.

Red sky at night, shepherds' delight. Red sky at morning, shepherds' warning.

Everyone is sociable until a cow invades their garden.

It's seldom a farm wife isn't involved on the farm. Whether it is feeding silage contractors or sheep shearers, keeping paperwork up to date, milking cows or just standing in a gap occasionally, there's usually some job you're asked to do. Whether you want to get away with doing less or would like to do more, here are some tips on making it easier as well as convincing all onlookers that you are a perfect farm wife.

WORKING ON THE FARM

If you were brought up on a farm, you may think you are well prepared for the farming life but every farmer and community has different ways of doing things. Sheep farming in the west is going to be completely different from dairy farming in the midlands or tillage farming in the east.

If you come from an urban background, don't worry: at least you haven't picked up any bad habits   just don't believe that his way of doing things is necessarily the best! This section will help you out with some of the more technical aspects to attaining perfect farm wife status.

How to be an efficient midwife

An important part of the farm cycle is the birth of livestock. You will definitely be called upon to assist at some stage. Sheep and goats often have multiple births. Twins are the most common (and are preferred from a manageability point of view), but they can have three, four or even five offspring. Your small hands and bucket loads of patience are required. Yes, that is why your small dainty hands received so much admiration on your first date. When there are multiples, their legs can get jumbled up with each other. It is a case of getting your hand in there to untangle them and give the mum a hand with delivering.

Cows usually have single calves but they can have complications occasionally. Normally a calf is born front feet first with the head and neck outstretched along the front legs, followed by the body and finally the back legs slide out. The most frequent complication is when a calf is coming backwards (back legs first). There is a risk of it smothering once the umbilical cord breaks so the birth has to be swift. That's why it is usually a two-person job: one to monitor the situation and ease the calf out, the other to work the calving aid when told to do so. Guess which one you'll be doing?

Once the calf is born, it may need some help with kick-starting its breathing. We hang the calf over a gate with its head hanging down, I hold onto its back legs to hold it in place while Brian rubs the chest to free the lungs of fluid and tickle its nose with straw to get it breathing. That usually does the trick, but sometimes it needs the kiss of life. Yes, it's fine to delegate this one to your husband. Alternatively, buy a resuscitation kit.

 The calving or lambing shed can be made very cosy. A few bales and an old blanket make a comfortable sofa at 3am when watching a mother progress. If the fridge is there for storing medicines, you could also store milk in it. All you need then is the kettle, a few mugs, teabags and a packet of biscuits! To be honest though, investing in modern technology such as calving cameras so the situation can be monitored from the comfort of the living room sofa is a much better idea.

How to feed lambs, kids and calves

Sheep and beef cows suckle their young so shouldn't require any intervention apart from monitoring. Dairy goat kids, the third and fourth born lambs and dairy calves are fed milk, and that's where you come in. Women have always been viewed as the better calf rearers and feeders of pet lambs, perhaps because of their allegedly more nurturing and patient nature. You are more patient than him, aren't you? As lambs and goat kids are small, they are easier to manage. Tuck a kid or lamb in under your arm and feed it with a bottle. It's quite relaxing to sit on a straw bale with a tiny lamb – with a radio in the shed to entertain you.

Calves are stronger and can be stubborn. You, as their surrogate mum, have to teach them how to drink from a bottle or a bucket. They can grasp the idea in minutes, but Sod's Law dictates they are very slow when you're tired or in a hurry.

In the 1860s, it was recommended that "if fed, calves should be fed four times a day for the first fortnight, a quart at a time".[28] That would be time-consuming! They are now fed twice a day unless they are poorly.

How to teach a calf to drink from a bucket

Scoop some milk into the calf's mouth. Once it gets the taste of the milk and is sucking on your fingers, move your fingers into the bucket to encourage the calf to dip its mouth in the milk. Remove your fingers as soon as possible or the calf will expect them to be there at every feed! This may have to be repeated a few times.

Happiness is when the calf grasps it within minutes. You must never be tempted to push the calf's head down into the bucket in an attempt to get it to drink. The calf will think it is going to drown and will head-butt you in the groin in response.

Most grasp it fairly quickly but there are always a few that refuse to take in sufficient milk no matter how many times you say "DRINK" with all the desperation and firmness of Father Jack.[29] I heard of a frustrated male farmer who finally threw a bucket of milk over a calf saying "It can bloody well soak in." You might come close but you'd never do that would you?

How to teach a calf to drink from a teat

Teaching them to drink from a teat is easier; it does mirror nature more effectively. Using a two-litre bottle, put the teat into the calf's mouth and hold the calf's head with your left hand. Once it gets the taste of the milk, it should suck steadily. If it doesn't, you could do with three hands: one to keep the head steady, one to prise open its mouth and one to hold the bottle. If the calf isn't obliging and keeps moving around, wedge it against a wall with your hip at its shoulder and use one hand to secure its head and open its mouth. If all else fails, you can feed it using a stomach tube.

Feed a stubborn or poorly calf in a pen on its own as otherwise the slightly older calves will turn their attention to you when they've drunk their milk. They think you are their mum, suck at your clothes and head-butt where they think the udder is. If one gets its head between your legs, you end up straddling a calf and hoping no one is watching.

As they are born without immunity, it is crucial they get the colostrum within two hours of birth, therefore you can't say "You'll bloody drink it later when you're hungry" and leave it until the next morning. It's like the scene from *Sex and the City* when Miranda is trying to feed Brady and she can't concentrate on anything until he has latched on and is drinking. It's not quite as bad when you're feeding a calf but I promise the same sense of relief does wash over you when it finally starts to suck.

Use teat feeders rather than buckets: it's easier. You'll have fewer problems with calves sucking on each other's navels too. Of course, if money is no object, buy an automatic feeder.

With dairy calves, try to feed them with the bottle for their first feed rather than letting them suck their mothers (unless born at 3am of course). If they suckle, they always seem to take longer to move from the bottle to the teat feeder. You'll also know exactly how much colostrum they have taken.

I doubt you can put an Aga down as a tax-deductible expense, but apparently they are wonderful at reviving tiny newborn lambs, should you need another reason to convince the farmer of its necessity in the new kitchen.

How to catch a calf

Calves are boisterous once they are a few days old and in the full of their health. When moving them from one shed to another, they either cavort around skittishly or refuse to move. You need to ensure there are no escape routes from the yard or you'll never get a frisky calf back!

One day I was sitting at my desk when I looked up and saw Brian at the bottom of the garden, trying desperately to hold onto a calf – by the tail! The calf had escaped while being moved to the calf shed and was running in circles around Brian. It was stone mad and strong! If it wasn't for the pained expression on Brian's face, you could be forgiven for thinking he was working up to swing the calf round and round in the air. Out I raced, although I was scarcely able to grab hold of anything as I was laughing so much. Brian was starting to lose his grasp on the tail so I grabbed the calf's two ears and held them long enough for Brian to tighten his grip. With us both holding onto an ear and with the other hand on its tail, we managed to get it back to the shed.

For that day when you might need to catch a calf, remember to grab a tail, an ear or a back leg. It can be a lot harder than it looks!

How to herd livestock

Herding (when you check the livestock to ensure all are healthy and none are missing) is a job that sounds easy enough. It looks like a pleasant stroll across the fields to check all livestock are present and correct before strolling back. There's a bit more to it than that, though. The first task is to count them. If there are over sixty animals, it can be a little tricky if they all look alike, bunch up together or keep moving around.

A competent farm wife is capable of counting them all in one go. You should be able to count in your head rather than having a finger poised in the air as you point at each animal and count aloud.

You need to check that they are all alert, that none have drooping ears, dull eyes, sore feet or swollen bellies. If a ewe is lying on its back, it could die; you need to pull or push her upright. If sheep have heavy fleeces, you also need to check them for maggots; signs include a twitching tail, a sheep trying to bite her flank or looking miserable and separated from the rest of the herd. The treatment is a bit grotesque: you cut off the affected wool, remove the maggots (yes, with your hands – bring gloves in a pocket) and pour some sheep dip over the lamb or ewe.

Don't be nervous when inquisitive cattle come close and sneak out a tongue to see if you are edible. It can be a little unnerving when heavy animals lumber along close behind you, so swish your arms behind you to keep them at a safe distance.

Never bring a yappy dog herding with you, especially if there are suckler cows with calves at foot. The cows might see the dog as a threat and attack both of you.

How to tell when an animal is fertile

Why on earth would you want to know this, I can hear you ask. While the birth of livestock is important, getting the conception right is doubly so.

Some farmers let nature take its course and use bulls, rams, boars and billy goats to father the young of their relevant livestock. Others use artificial insemination (purchased semen from a variety of high-quality sires) to improve the quality and genetic diversity of the herd or flock. The aim is to get the majority inseminated within a six-week period. It is hugely important that each heat cycle is noted and the female is "served". In dairy herds, each cow's missed heat costs up to €250 between the loss of milk and the calf being born later, so it is worth your while to be observant. Unfortunately, the €250 doesn't materialise the next spring when the calf is born on time, so you can't reward yourself with new shoes.

When an animal is fertile, she displays particular behaviour. I'm so glad humans aren't as obvious about it! If it is your turn to enjoy the voyeuristic pastime of observing them, you'll find that some signs aren't so noticeable and others are right in your face! They include being noisy; walking around briskly; perked ears; a mucus discharge; jumping on her friends or standing still when another fertile comrade jumps on her. You have to be sharp-eyed and make a note of the behaviour and the ear tag numbers of those on heat.

Was it easier half a century ago, before artificial insemination became so popular? No – most farmers didn't have stock bulls and had to bring cows and heifers on heat to a neighbour's farm to be served by their bull. Walking a lone animal in a highly strung state across fields with little fencing and along a road for two miles was not for the faint-hearted!

If you're not so keen on observing them so frequently, utilise some other methods too. Choose between tail painting, putting patches on their backs (both of which will let you know if the animals have been mounting each other) or a monitor around their necks to detect changes in behaviour.

How to bring cows in to be milked

Bringing cows in for milking is a perfect excuse for an evening stroll. It's a nice way to spend time with your beloved too. However, if you are on your own, and the cows aren't familiar with you, they may toss their heads and resolve to stay where they are. If you don't have the cattle dog with you, this job might take some time. Cows can be lazy about coming in, particularly if their bellies are full with good grass. They are chewing their cud, feeling sanguine and relaxed. They are not in the mood to walk to the yard, stand in a queue, be milked and walk back to the field again. It would be like asking you to do a supermarket shop when you're lying on a sun lounger with a glass of wine and a good book.

Once you do manage to persuade them to get to their feet, they always have a long toilet break. Step back or you'll be splashed!

As they amble towards the gate, don't forget to see if any are displaying signs of being on heat.

Use bringing in the cows as an opportunity to get into their relaxed zone. I think it's one of the nicest jobs on the farm (as long as the flies aren't out in force).

How to milk cows

Women have long been considered to be better than men at milking cows. The importance of using skilled operators for milking cows is emphasised in this quote from the 1860s:

> The art of milking is not taught in a hurry. A good milker obtains at least a quart more from the same cow as a poor milker. They should be taught to milk as fast as possible. No conversation must be permitted in the milk yard. A savage, ill-tempered milker will often spoil a cow. Women are by far the most capable of milking, their hands are more gentle and delicate, and the cows seem to prefer them.[30]

My paternal grandmother was reported to be a better milker than my grandfather. She "could make a hole in the bucket" such was the force of the stream of milk hitting the bottom of the pail when she was milking.

The milking of cows was often idealised in paintings and poetry: pretty milkmaids walking with a yoke over their shoulders and two buckets to milk cows in a distant flower-strewn meadow. I'm not sure how they managed to carry their milking stools too. They leaned their heads against warm flanks as the rich creamy goodness flowed into the buckets. There was little mention of wet dew, cross cows that kicked or the weight of the buckets of milk. However, it was accurate that in the mid nineteenth century, cows were sometimes milked in the field. It was believed that "milk was wasted if cows were walked from a field to the yard for milking",[31] hence women did the walking and carrying instead.

Women and children transported churns to the local creamery or up a lane for a roadside collection. Milk had to be ready earlier on a Sunday morning as the collection was earlier. Some got up at 5am to have it ready in time; others churned the weekend milk into butter for home use and for sale into shops.

Women's work was respected and appreciated, if not by their significant others, then in some writing of the day as early as a century ago. This writer credited women and children with the success and continuation of dairy farms.

Freeman's Journal 13 November 1919

Where there were thirty cows in a dairy in Tipperary, there were none now. He defied any farmer who had not a family to help him run a farm of dairy cows now.

Of 408 husbands interviewed in 1979, 67% said it would be impossible to manage without the help of a wife in the farm business.[32]

The average size of a dairy herd in Ireland is now sixty-five cows and many farmers are expanding each year. Milking is a two-person job in larger milking parlours. Look on it as a way to spend quality time together! The good news is you don't have to use a milking stool and spend ten minutes hand-milking each cow. The bad news is your head is positioned just under a cow's tail when putting the cluster on the teats.

Cows like routine, so if the milking is similar every day they are happy. They don't like strangers or loud voices and will react by defecating, usually when you are nearby. They like coming into the parlour in their own designated space. Some insist on being the first cow in a row, others prefer anywhere in the middle. If a cow ends up in a place where she isn't comfortable, she becomes nervous and agitated. She probably won't let down her milk but will definitely defecate. She may even cough while doing so, which means it is delivered with considerable force and surprisingly good aim at the humans.

You should get to know your cows by recognising their udder markings as well as the numbers on ear tags. Freeze branding is helpful!

When putting the clusters on the udder, let your hands find the teats rather than sticking your head in close to the udder. You risk being kicked in the face if you do that.

Milking together can test and probably strengthen your relationship. You will find out how considerate he is if he points out the cows most likely to kick or spray you with excrement.

Don't take on milking on your own as once he sees you are competent at it, he may head off to do the "important jobs" of going to the evening mart or to herd (and chat to other farmers). Let him feel he is in charge of the milking!

You're now an Udder Master, a Milk Procurement Manager or a Bovine Lactation Consultant – take your pick!

How to keep hens

Years ago, all farm wives kept hens. Many earned an essential income from the production of eggs. Unless you have a few hens, you may not be considered a true farm wife! It won't be too taxing – four hens will supply sufficient eggs for the family. A chicken coop with a run is ideal but a small shed is fine if you're letting them roam around the farmyard. They require straw, a nesting box, a bar to roost on and a door that fastens at night to keep predators out.

Rhode Island Reds are excellent layers and easy to look after. Keep them in their shed for a week so they learn to recognise it as their home. You can then let them out mid morning (once they have laid their eggs) and shut them in before dusk. Mr Fox does his rounds as dusk approaches, but that doesn't mean he or his wife will not be about at other times, especially in the summer when they have young.

Feed your hens with layers pellets, cooked potato skins, vegetable peelings, leftover pasta and rice. Give them grit and a supply of clean water. They will repay you with an egg each most days.

Hens have great personalities; and don't worry, no one will think you are mad if you have a conversation with them. Always remember to thank them for their eggs. I love seeing them pecking around the farmyard. All I have to do is call "henny, henny" and they come running. They cluck with appreciation for leftovers but give muted clucks of disapproval for layers pellets. Hens are the easiest providers of food – they don't have to be milked or shorn or slaughtered!

I thought I had lost a hen to the fox some time ago; she was missing for ten days. We were scanning cows one day when a hen emerged from the straw bales in the hayshed. She tottered out, drank about half a pint of water from a puddle before I scooped her up and put her back in their house with some food. The poor thing had gone in amongst the bales and got lost in what was, to her, a maze.

Having a good working dog will help to keep the fox at bay. Yet again, the dog is worth his weight in gold.

Buy your hens from a reputable seller. Hen rescue centres sell hens too; these hens have finished their time on an intensive farm. By giving them a good retirement, they will repay you with plenty of eggs.

When the children outgrow the sand in their sandbox, the hens will love it as they need grit.

How to hug a cow

Would you believe that hugging a cow could be big business? City people in some European countries, particularly Holland, spend good money to hug a cow. The cows are trained to sit quietly while the humans breathe in their smell and sit ensconced in their aura.

If you want to try it at home, go into a field of cows (checking there's no bull there first) and sit on the grass. Cows are curious creatures. After a minute or two of looking at you, they will come up to investigate and snake out a long tongue. If they lick your face or hand, you'll discover that lengthy tongue feels like exceedingly rough sandpaper. Most will back off if you try to hug them though. It takes time and patience!

We had Hereford Friesian calves this year for the first time. They are quite happy to be rubbed down or hugged; they are much less wary than the Friesians. I prefer when they are a little suspicious as playfulness can be dangerous as they get older. A weanling calf could think it is having fun yet could send you flying.

 If trying to hug a cow, don't do it in public view of the road: other farmers will think you are bonkers.

How to care for goats

If you decide to try goat farming, work on your fencing skills first. You need strong and secure fencing as goats have extreme escapist tendencies, worse even than sheep. They eat anything and everything. That includes the flowers in your garden, the leaves from trees and even the clothes from your line.

Goats don't like getting wet. They need shelter as they can catch colds or pneumonia. The first year we had our two goats, Becky and Megan, we set up an old large kennel in the field as their shelter. We thought they would both step in, but no, bossy Becky stood in the doorway and left Megan standing outside in the rain. So we had to do something about that!

They were in a paddock by day and a shed at night. One day I could not get Becky to go into their field. All other three goats were in there and she just refused. I ran her back to a different shed and locked her in for the day. "That'll teach you!" I told her as she tossed her head, shook her beard and smiled at me – or maybe the baring of her teeth was a grimace. She looked rather pleased with herself when I let her out later; I presumed it was because of her stubbornness in not giving in to me. But she had the last laugh – I didn't know Brian had left a half-full bag of calf meal in the corner and she had found it. No wonder she was smug!

Even though they had a makeshift hut in the field, they preferred to race to our garden when it rained and shelter in the large open porch. One day I answered the doorbell to see a friend running back to her car. Her two children were sitting in the back seat looking terrified and the four goats were standing guard at the front door.

Bringing them to the billy goat can be an experience. Our goat always seemed to go on heat on dark, wet, busy November days. We didn't have a small trailer so had to load her into the back of the van. When the van "died", she went in the boot of our "new" farm car. Then there was the experience of feeling like a peeping Tom while she got it on with a billy goat.

 Use treats to bribe your goats, especially at milking time. Never buy a goat that is smarter or more stubborn than you!

How to move livestock along the road

All self-respecting farmers' wives have to be able to stop a gap. This means standing in an open gateway or at the end of a road to prevent animals going in that direction. If it's not a wide gap, you may just have to stand there so the livestock see you and trot past. If it is wide or the animals are skittish, wave a stick and make yourself look as big as possible.

Due to the fragmented nature of Ireland's farms, moving livestock across or along a stretch of road is commonplace. When the day dawns, ensure you have all the necessary paraphernalia. These are: a belt on your trousers to keep them up, wellies, a good sports bra, a stick and your mobile phone. You never know when you might have to communicate with your other half. Wear a reflector vest so drivers see you in plenty of time. The stick is not to be used to hit the animals but to elongate your arms or wave it at them. It has a use for humans too which you'll see below.

If you are behind the animals, make sure any "stragglers" keep up with the others. If they have time to think and the fencing is poor, it multiples the chances of them jumping the hedge into the adjoining field.

If any heifers are on heat, be prepared to act quickly as they can be somewhat hormonal and erratic and could jump over hedges if the notion takes them. Keep them bunched together if you can.

Should any drivers become impatient, just smile and wave as if saying "it will only be another minute". If they get really annoyed and look like they are considering overtaking the livestock, raise your stick high in the air and scowl. A pitchfork works even better but can be awkward to carry if you're running along. When the animals go into their field and the drivers accelerate, always smile and call "thank you". Give yourself a clap on the back too.

 Train the animals so they think any wire will give them an electric shock. They should stay clear of wire tied temporarily across open gateways then. This will save you having to be in half a dozen places at once.

Don't use your phone for non-essential reasons when moving cattle. Forget about taking photos for Instagram and Twitter too. If something goes wrong, you'll get the blame for not paying attention.

How to sort a batch of animals into two groups

Sorting livestock means dividing them into two groups. Male and female calves need to be separated; lambs are divided according to size and ewes are sorted depending on how many lambs they are carrying.

As each ewe is scanned, she is colour-coded by being sprayed with a dye. For example, those carrying single lambs are sprayed with red spray and those carrying twins are sprayed in blue. You need to know how many lambs there are because mothers carrying triplets or quads need more food during pregnancy. It may be your job to stand in the gateway while your partner tries to send the singles towards you to let through. If a ewe pregnant with more than one lamb heads in your direction, wave your stick and send her back to the group.

Depending on the breed of cattle, they can look very similar. Friesians have varying degrees of black and white. As the farmer knows them well, he relies on his descriptive powers of "the black one", "the whitest one" and "THAT ONE, THAT ONE". Unfortunately, his opinion of "the blackest one" can differ from yours. There's lots of shouting if the wrong one is let through. Never fret too much if that happens. Yes, it's a pain having to get her back but it's not the end of the world. Ensure he knows the mistake was down to his poor communication skills rather than your misinterpretation.

 If you're a cattle farmer, follow the sheep farmers' example. If running the cattle through the chute (cattle crush) to vaccinate them before separating them, spray the males with a coloured dot. It makes sorting them a lot easier than trying to see between their legs when they are coming towards you. It also reduces the shouting and swearing between the humans.

You could threaten to leave him to it if he curses. You only have to follow through once and he'll know in future that you mean it.

How to deal with death on the farm

The expression "where there is livestock, there is deadstock" is used to console you if you are upset about an animal dying. It might be true but is rarely of real comfort. Many people think it is strange that farmers are saddened when an animal dies as of course we do send animals to the factory.

There is an element of Sod's Law when it comes to your animals dying before their time: it always seems to be the best calf or a favourite cow. You are genuinely upset when it happens as well as annoyed if you feel you could have done more. We lost a cow named Daisy last year. We don't name many cows but she had a special personality. She had great character; was slightly clumsy, a little bit bolshy and she delivered twins the first time she calved, which meant we were always going to have a soft spot for her. Brian was going out along the car road (cow track) to shut the gate on their field after milking and discovered Daisy standing near the gate. He knew instantly she wasn't well. In the minute it took him to ring the vet, she had given two bellows and dropped down dead. She had milked fine an hour before. For it to happen so suddenly, it must have been a heart attack. Naming them definitely makes it harder if they die. However, she had a heifer calf that year so we are looking forward to Daisyella coming into the milking herd next spring.

Farm animals are collected by the animal collection service. Although very upset if a favourite dies, children are often quite matter-of-fact about animal deaths. There was one occasion when we lost a calf when the children were five and three. I was telling Kate that a sick calf had died and gone to heaven when Will ran out of the shed and overheard us. "No, he hasn't gone yet," he called over. "He's still lying in the shed."

 The death of farm animals teaches children (and adults) about the cycle of life, to understand pain does ease with time and the quality of life is highly important too.

ADDING TO YOUR TECHNICAL KNOW-HOW

Farming is very scientific now. Farmers are constantly working out how best to react to changing weather conditions to get the best yield from crops. They look for the optimum condition on all livestock. Whether it is choosing the best sires for the females, selecting replacement stock, improving grass management, or changing their system to maximise profits, every year brings its challenges. A farmer is always learning something new.

How to measure grass

Some farmers measure grass weekly to ensure it is at its most nutritious when the livestock are eating it. If it gets too long or stemmy, the feeding value is reduced. You don't require a ruler or measuring tape but it's not far off. You need a quadrant, clippers, weighing scales and plastic bags to weigh the grass and work out kg of dry matter per hectare. (For example, a cow eats 17 kg of dry matter in 24 hours.) Bring your tablet to record the information so you can plan your grass management later.

Having conversations about how many kg of grass are in the fields makes for exciting conversations once a week. You will hear him talking about his wedge and the rotation quite a lot! You definitely won't need a gym membership if you are going to be striding around the farm with your grass measuring paraphernalia. Get a pedometer and impress your friends when you reveal you walk 20,000 steps on your grass measuring days.

Spare a little time for romance. While the fields won't be flower-strewn meadows at the time you need to measure grass, you can at least go to do it together.

How to drive a tractor and reverse a trailer

Good driving skills are a must for a competent farm wife. Few rural women were able to drive years ago. The farmer drove her to town to do the shopping while he went to the pub. Farmers' wives now whizz into town for emergency spare parts and squeeze in a quick grocery shop while they are there.

Being able to drive tractors, quads and loaders is more important if the farm is fragmented. One person can drive the tractor over to the out-farm and the other brings the loader if both are needed. Your farm tasks might include spreading fertiliser or bringing lambs to the mart. Even if you aren't keen on tractor driving, it's good to know you are capable in case your beloved breaks a leg or something.

Reversing a trailer is an advanced skill in my opinion. It is one thing to drive a tractor but quite another when there's a trailer or a slurry spreader behind it. If bringing calves or lambs to the mart, men seem to find it amusing to watch a woman reverse but get bored very quickly once she proves she is competent.

To reverse with a trailer, you need to turn the steering wheel in the opposite direction you want the trailer to go. The difficulty arises if you turn too tight and the trailer almost goes at a right angle to your vehicle – it can even cause damage to it. Lots of practice in a wide open field is advised. Just ensure you are on your own, with no one to observe or pass comment.

If you don't want to provide the other mart goers with entertainment, don't feel any shame in asking one of them to reverse it for you. He'll feel good about being a knight in shining armour.

How to interpret sign language

There are plenty of times when you just can't hear each other (which is not always a bad thing!). Maybe you are moving cattle along the road, he at the front and you bringing up the rear, and something goes awry. Maybe he is on the tractor trying to warn you about a gate being open. Maybe a cow has unexpectedly calved in the field, the calf has fallen down a dyke and he needs help getting it out. Using the phone isn't always an option. He can see you so he thinks you can interpret his sign language and loud shouts. It is not easy trying to understand incomprehensible yells and waving arms, especially when you're tempted to return hand gestures of your own. When you see arms flung up into the air, you know it has gone past the stage of no return.

Whatever you do, don't surprise him with a picnic lunch and on arriving at the field decide to drive across it at speed. His enthusiastic waving might not indicate his pleasure at seeing you but be to warn you of the large hole at the midway point of the field – a hole that isn't obvious by any markings except the pile of earth beside it. If seeing a pile of earth as a danger signal isn't on your radar, you'll need the help of the tractor to pull you out.

 You know the failed communication is due to his impatience but I wouldn't risk telling him that. Planning some communication training is a good idea. The dog manages with a few commands such as "sit", "come bye", "away" and "that'll do". I'm not suggesting you bark instructions at each other but the following signs might help:

- Arm pointing in a particular direction means "Go over there."
- Arm raised with the palm of the hand showing means "Stop."
- Waving at you means "Come on quickly."

What does he really mean?

Make sure you can translate his comments, as they will often have deeper meanings than it would appear.

- "Can I have a hand for a few minutes?" *This may take some time.*
- "Um, are you busy today?" *I have a job I need help with and it might take till teatime.*
- "Are you going to town someday soon?" *Today would be handy as I have a shopping list for you as long as your arm.*
- "Have you any spare dinner do you think?" *The contractors are on their way and will be here in time for dinner – all eight of them. I may have forgotten to mention it.*
- "Will we go for a drive on Sunday?" Is he proposing to stop off at a nice country pub and go for a leisurely walk? Hmmm, no. You'll be the chauffeur while he peers over the hedges to see what the grass or crops are like. The conversation will be a running commentary on the fields. If he meets another farmer, you'll have to stop so they can chat away about farming. Having you with him means people won't see him as being nosy; everyone will think he is out for a Sunday drive!
- "Pick up a bunch of pigtails when you're in town." He's not asking for some strange hair accessory but a bunch of temporary fencing stakes, so called as the top is like the curl on a pig's tail. They are used with electric wire to divide a field temporarily.
- "Can you give me a hand drawing cattle this afternoon?" No, he's not proposing that you both head to a hillside with your watercolours, but that he will be bringing (drawing) cattle in a cattle trailer from one part of the farm to another.
- "Check the triplets this afternoon." It's unlikely you'll find batches of triplet lambs in the field. Triplets refer to ewes pregnant with triplets and he wants you to check in case any are in labour.
- "Is dinner ready yet?" *Can I have my dinner right now?*

Always barter: "Yes, I can come out and help for a minute; will you put up that shelf this evening?" Or "Yes, I can pop into town and collect them; can you get in early tomorrow night as I'm going out with the girls?"

How to become a weather girl

For most city people, it's important the weather is good when they are off work at the weekends. They want to get out into the garden, go for walks or bring kids to activities. If the weather is hot and dry, their biggest concern is watering garden plants and flowers.

When your livelihood is largely dependent on Mother Nature and Father Time, very dry or very wet weather affects your annual income. If the harvest is of high quality, helped by good weather, it saves some expense the following winter. If the weather stays fine late into the autumn, livestock can stay out eating grass rather than being moved indoors to eat expensive silage and meal. Watching the weather forecast becomes an engrained habit; your children shout out "The weather forecast is on" from about the age of four!

According to those living in towns, rain is either light rain or heavy rain. For farmers, there's a vast difference in the type of rain that falls. As a farm wife, you learn how to decipher if a particular type of rain falling is positive or negative on any specific day. Mist on one day might be just what is needed, but if he is making hay, it is exactly what he doesn't want.

Allegedly the Inuit have forty terms for snow. Do the Irish come close with their terms for rain? Farmers use most of these to describe the vagaries of precipitation:

◢ *A grand soft day:* A mild day where the rain is so soft, it feels like it is barely touching your skin. The moisture and the heat are perfect for growing grass.

◢ *Soft:* Soft rain (but without the heat of "a grand soft day").

◢ *Mist:* Often with fog, a grey mist is when the rain just hangs in the air, yet everything is soaked.

◢ *Drizzle:* Similar to a mist but when the rain is actually falling rather than hanging in the air. You can become very wet in a surprisingly short time.

◢ *Spitting rain:* When it seems as if the clouds are trying to rain harder but can't quite manage it. Spitting rain is similar in volume to drizzle but the drops are larger and can hurt as they are almost spiky!

◢ *Showers:* Heavy rain in relatively short bursts.

◢ *A cloudburst:* A quick sharp shower usually preceded and followed by bright sunshine. You're rewarded with a rainbow.

◢ *April showers:* Multiple sudden showers separated by bright sunshine (not limited to April).

◢ *A bit of a squib:* When the clouds attempt to shower but aren't capable and very little rain actually falls. This term is used when the farm needs rain and farmers are disgusted that the promised shower was "only a bit of a squib".

◢ *Trying to rain:* The farmer is usually looking for rain when this happens. The air is heavy, there's thunder in the air, a storm seems imminent, and he is looking towards the sky waiting for clouds to open.

◢ *Driving rain:* This is rain that lashes hard against the windscreen or window, driving down with diagonal lines.

◢ *Lashing rain:* Heavy rain but it falls in straighter lines than driving rain.

◢ *Pouring rain:* Heavy rain pours out of the heavens and saturates you to the skin.

◢ *Drenching rain:* Such a heavy shower, it soaks you in seconds. Drenching rain is much heavier than pouring rain.

◢ *Chucking it down:* When it rains so heavily the gutters overflow and large puddles form in minutes. It rains so hard it is similar to being doused with a bucket of cold water.

◢ *A sudden downpour:* The clue is in the adjective; downpours are often sudden and will just soak everything within minutes. A downpour is much heavier than a shower. When it stops, rain may be running off the yard. Similar to "chucking it down" but of shorter duration.

◢ *Torrential rain:* This is heavier than a downpour and longer lasting; rainwater flows down the yard like a river. You look like a "drowned rat" if you are caught out in this.

◢ *Sleety rain:* Rain that is very cold; not quite cold enough to be snow or hail but horrible. It feels like pins on your face.

◢ *Thunder shower:* A heavy shower of rain when the air is warm and humid. The shower clears the air and makes it fresher.

You'll be a figure of fun if you use an umbrella on the farm. Farmers either stand under a tree to shelter during a quick shower, decide to do paperwork in the house for the afternoon if the rain is heavy, or just get on with it and wear a raincoat.

UTILISING YOUR EXISTING SKILLS

Remember I said not to worry if you didn't have any experience of farming? Well, one of the reasons is you will find plenty of opportunities to use your existing skills and previous experience to make life more efficient on the farm. Believe me, every one of them will come in handy.

Your version of agrifashion

Would you believe that getting rid of their cow was the first step some Donegal women took in terms of improving their appearance? It was the early 1960s, husbands were working abroad most of the year and the women had to weed the crops, milk the cow and harvest hay, turnips and potatoes for fodder for the winter. When the milkman arrived offering bottles of milk, it took time (and lots of gossip when the first woman sold her cow) but one by one, many women made the decision to sell their single cow and buy the milk.

> "You would know the women in the chapel on Sunday that had got rid of the cows," she said. "Their faces were not as haggard or as weather-beaten from being out in the fields. They didn't have as many wrinkles.

That was when married women and older women took interest in their appearance. The milk changed our lives."[33]

From that situation fifty years ago we now have the Best Dressed Lady competitions at shows and the races. You might be there in your overcoat and boots and wonder how the poor dears are surviving in their silk dresses, huge headpieces and stilettos. More sensibly, agricultural shows now have Most Appropriately Dressed Lady competitions too – do you think you would stand a chance of winning?

There is nothing wrong with celebrating your femininity. The cows or sheep won't mind what you wear so if you feel happier wearing lip gloss and nail varnish, go for it. Comfortable wellies, shapely jeans with a belt, shirt and snug jacket indicate you are a fashionable and sensible farm wife. He made a "good catch"!

There are times when you'll feel like you have been pulled through a hedge backwards, and probably look like you have too. If nipping to the local shop in the winter months, it's easy enough to cover up unruly hair with a hat, boots can replace wellies and a long coat covers a multitude. It's not so easy in the summer though. Don't ignore bright colours either. My pink wellies make me smile. I love seeing my daughter wearing bright colours out on the farm, with her long copper hair flying back as she runs along. (Don't worry, it's a myth that bulls are enraged by the colour red.)

If you do need to change from work clothes to looking more respectable if someone comes to the door, you need to be able to do that quickly. Whether it's a stranger arriving at the hall door, an important unexpected visitor like the priest or clergyman, or a salesperson, you know you'll be taken more seriously when you look, well, slightly groomed.

Don't wear a scarf around your neck. It's dangerous as it can catch in things and could strangle you. Take all cords out of clothing too, for example, the cords in raincoats.

Never ever just nip up the yard in your best jeans to check on something – that is the time that something happens and splatters them with muck. Sod's Law again.

How to run fast in wellies

Can you run in heels? If so, you might be able to outrun cattle when wearing wellies. If livestock escape from their field, you might have to sprint over high grassy tussocks, through wet tall grass destined for silage or across a neighbour's fields. You have to be a couple of kilometres an hour faster than the escaped beast. There's a Sod's Law to this. As you start to speed up, the cow will go faster. If you jog, it will trot. If you trot, it will canter. If you canter, it will gallop.

In Castlecomer, Co. Kilkenny, the ability to run in wellies is so well respected that there is a 10km run in wellies every New Year's Day. Come along and get some practice in!

Invest in a good working dog. If you're not married yet, buy your fiancé one as a wedding present. If it is a good worker, it'll be the best gift you ever bought ~~yourself~~ him. Invest in a trained dog – there's no point having a dog and doing the barking yourself.

How to use your hairdressing skills

If you have ever worked as a beautician or hairdresser, you can use those skills again to clip cows' tails and dag sheep. You don't want a long stringy tail slapping you in the face when you're milking cows. The ewes need the wool at their back ends trimmed from time to time, especially before mating and before they give birth. You can wear gloves to protect your hands and using a shears or clippers, get stuck in. It's quite a satisfying job once you stand back to admire your handiwork.

Your skills will definitely be put to good use if you show animals at the agricultural shows. Between shampooing, brushing, clipping and adding tail extensions, it can be a full-time job.

Keep all sharp knives and scissors under lock and key in the house or ensure they have bright pink handles so he doesn't "borrow" them to use up the yard for a few minutes. "Borrowing" means if you ever see them again, they will be tarnished and rusty from the rain, never mind needing to be sterilised.

How to keep your hands soft

Farmers' hands tend to be much larger than other men's hands. Have you noticed? Between cold weather, hard work and getting wet, hands become deeply lined and cracked, and stained with dark brown. Welts and blister scars take months to disappear. Your hands will end up with the same fate if you don't take care of them. Wear gloves for many jobs, especially milking, and use a good hand cream.

Being a sheep farmer can have its advantages as the lanolin in the fleeces will keep your hands soft if you handle them. You probably won't be shearing, as many farmers hire professional sheep shearers if the flock is large, but that doesn't mean you get away scot free. Your jobs will be cooking dinner for the shearers as well as handling (sometimes classifying) the wool. Being a wool handler involves gathering up the fleeces, removing any dirty bits, rolling them up and putting each one neatly into a huge sack. You also have to keep the area clean. It is hot and sweaty work!

If your hands get really mucky, sprinkle baby oil and sugar into your gloves to do the next job, and your hands will be cleansed as you work. Nail varnish can cover those engrained stains and marks on your nails!

How to find the right field

If you worked in sales and travelled around the country, you may consider yourself to be good at map-reading, or at least capable of knowing if the map reader is sending you in the best direction. What about orienteering on farms?

Nearly every field on a farm is named. Some are named after farmers from long ago. Others are named according to their shape or size. Some even have history in the name. One of our fields is named after a convicted murderer! The farmer knows the field names as well as he knows the names of any of his friends but it can take some time for you to familiarise yourself with them. Learn the names that apply to shape and size first. These may include Long Meadow, Big Field, Round Field and the Hill Field. Then work on those named for something in or beside the field: Road Field, Buttercup Field, Heathery Hill, Quarry Field, Chapel Field, The Letterbox. Some have very practical if less romantic names: The Field with the Hole, the Field beside the Yard, the Field behind the House, the Field in front of the House – you get the picture! By the way, there is nearly always a field called The Bog – the wettest field on the farm.

It's worse when fields don't have names. You'll need a good sense of direction when you get instructions to go to "the field that's above the third field over, but you can't access it that way so you'll have to go up two paddocks and then over diagonally to the third field on the left, the one with the gorse in the hedge". They probably all have gorse in the hedge, but you need all your observational skills to realise that field has more than the others.

Livestock farmers tend to think that tillage farmers have an easy life. All they have to do is sit on a tractor and drive. That's true, but the hours can be considerable if it's a large farm. You'll be busy too. Your jobs include driving machinery; collecting spare parts and delivering meals to wherever the farmers are working. This means finding your way around. If your husband is a contractor, you have the added challenge of remembering the names of other farmers' fields too.

 If you've been told to bring food or spare parts to a particular field, give yourself plenty of time and don't get flustered. Take the male approach: you never get lost, you were just taking your time.

How to be prepared for all events

Cows, cattle or sheep (or whatever livestock you have) always seem to know the worst day to break out of their field. When a special day is coming up, you need to be prepared for any eventuality. Wedding planning has nothing on pre-empting the escapist goals of wayward sheep. Planning a lie on or a night out? Yes, the animals will break out.

One morning at 7am I was dimly aware of the radio alarm being on and then I heard Brian shouting for me. Some of the 90 calves we put in a field the day before had broken out – they must have been spooked during the night – and some were on the road. "They broke the wire; I had to put up gates to stop the rest getting out," he shouted, "I rang the landline three times and your mobile twice. How come you always have that phone with you except when I need you?" As my brain was taking this in, I was working out what to wear. Should I leave on my pyjamas? Probably not if I was going to be running along the road. Did I have time to put on a bra? No. Where were my jeans? No sign of them so better pull on leggings. In the end, I ran down the stairs in leggings and a t-shirt, grabbed a jacket to hide my bra-lessness and pulled on wellies as I ran out the door.

We drove around and found three calves on a by-road nearby, lying down by a gateway. They just looked at me as if to say, "Are you really going to make us move?" They were quite happy to walk, rather than run, back to our gateway. Seventeen were dotted around three fields and the other seventy were fast asleep at the top of their field. Thankfully we got them all safely back. You just never know what is going to happen next.

Ensure that the landline phone has a loud ringtone, particularly if you are in the habit of leaving your mobile phone in the living area at night.

Always have your farm clothes ready in case of an emergency.

How to enjoy living on the farm

Some women get a bit fed up living on a farm. Reasons include underestimating the amount of work, being nervous of working with animals, feeling inadequate when completing some farm tasks, feeling under-appreciated, over-worked, underpaid and sometimes lonely too.

Farming is a business and as part-owner of that business, you're a strong and efficient businesswoman, able to kick ass if necessary. Remember to avoid the negativity and embrace the positives. Apply your existing skills to farming, delegate the jobs you ~~detest~~ don't have time for, and become a perfect farm wife with aplomb.

Being too good at a task means there is a strong chance it becomes one of your permanent jobs so ensure you like it before you excel! Successful and happy family farming is all about teamwork and equality. If you are sharing the farm jobs, get him to help inside even if you have to leave written instructions every time you want the floor swept and washed. You know you're a true farmer when you get more job satisfaction from cleaning calf feeders than washing your kitchen floor!

Just as a problem shared is a problem halved, you'll get twice the pleasure and satisfaction when you both share dreams and work to see them fulfilled.

Don't forget to make time to celebrate. Embrace what the farm has to offer and enjoy. We only get one stab at life so get down and dirty in your farming clothes, making the most of your "good life".

FARM WIFE QUIZ (2)

1. The calving/lambing season is starting next week. What do you add to the shopping list:
    (a) Chocolate, tea, iodine, baking ingredients, gloves, batteries and washing powder
    (b) Whatever he told you to buy
    (c) Earplugs?

2. He comes in freezing cold at 4am having been up calving cows and lambing sheep. Do you:
    (a) Move your body closer to his so he can avail of your body warmth
    (b) Move to the edge of the bed so you aren't affected by the icy air around him
    (c) Not wake up at all?

3. You are replacing your front door. What do you decide to do with the old wooden one? Do you:
    (a) Decide it will be a perfect gate or partial fence in one of the fields or sheds
    (b) Put it in the shed as it might come in useful someday
    (c) Get the installer of the new door to take it away?

4. It's time for your favourite old cow to go to the factory. Do you:
   (a) Get upset but realise it's time and let her go
   (b) Decide to give her one more year and hope she has a heifer calf so you can keep her
   (c) Refuse to let her go and vow to let her retire on the farm for as long as she lives?

5. He asks you to help him draw cattle to the out-farm. Do you:
   (a) Put aside a few hours and don your wellies
   (b) Remind yourself to buy him a working dog for his birthday
   (c) Go and find your easel and watercolours?

6. You are buying a dress in a boutique and open your handbag to take out your purse. Something falls and as someone bends down to pick it up for you, you realise it's a:
   (a) Thermometer with 'Calf' written on it
   (b) Cheque book with dubious stains all over it
   (c) Your manicure set?

7. What are the essentials in your calving/lambing/kidding shed?
   (a) Calving ropes, calving jack, iodine, lubricant, gloves, warm water, disinfectant, extra straw, stomach tube feeder, clean buckets and bottles, ear tags and tagger, notebook or phone for recording details
   (b) Resuscitation kit – you don't want to have to give a calf or lamb the kiss of life
   (c) Where's the calving shed?

8. A hen is not giving eggs any more. Do you:
   (a) Wring its neck, pluck it, clean it out and put her in the pot, just like your grandmother did
   (b) Let her enjoy her retirement, she can die of old age and natural causes
   (c) Let your husband deal with it as you don't want to know?

9. You get a call from a neighbour to say your heifers are in their small field at the end of their garden but they will put them back in your field for you:
   (a) You know instantly that they aren't cows, they are thirty yearling bulls and tell them to say inside, you'll be over in a few minutes
   (b) You tell them to wait until you get over but the help would be great
   (c) You say thank you very much and forget to mention it to your farmer?

10. The price of your farm product (milk, beef, lamb, grain) hits an all-time low this year. Do you:
    (a) Shrug and say 'at least there will be less going to the Revenue'
    (b) Resolve to spend a bit less on shoes this year
    (c) Curse the day that you married a farmer?

How did you do?

Mostly A's – Wow, you're impressive. You have your finger on the pulse. You're realistic yet optimistic. Perfect indeed.

Mostly B's – You're good. Efficient, frugal and yet not afraid to spend money where it's needed.

Mostly C's – Hmmm, keep reading, you'll get there.

PART FOUR

THE FARM HOUSEHOLD

The model farmhouse, as demonstrated in glossy magazines, has clean wellies lined up at the back door, coats hanging on rurally themed hooks, walking sticks in a corner, groomed dog at the door and a cat curled up on a rocking chair by the Aga. The smell of fresh baking wafts around the kitchen. The farmer's wife looks attractive wearing fashionable jeans and boots, a white shirt and tweed jacket, pearl earrings and holding a couple of perfectly shaped logs for the stove.

HOW CLEAN IS YOUR HOUSE?

Maintaining a clean farmhouse can be a challenge particularly if it is situated in the middle of the yard with farm vehicles driving past, sending up dust to dirty your clean windows. A farmhouse kitchen can be a far cry from a high-gloss bespoke and sparklingly gleaming kitchen in a townhouse. Townhouse utility rooms serve as laundry rooms and an exit to the back garden. Farmhouse ones are multi-functional: yes, they are laundry rooms, but also a space to kick off mucky boots, remove dirty overalls, store numerous coats, stash implements being repaired and, of course, the windowsill displays all the oddments from trouser pockets.

Never apologise to visitors if the house is untidy, you are only bringing attention to it. If they have witnessed it being clean and tidy on other occasions, they understand it is a busy time. They may even be relieved to see you are human and a tad messy! As long as you have some home baking to offer them, they'll be happy. (There's more on home baking later.)

How to keep the farmhouse clean

Let's start by admitting it's not easy to keep a farmhouse clean, not if you're working on the farm and have a busy family life. It is a working building with people going in and out all the time. You go to town leaving a tidy house and you never quite know what you are coming home to. The kitchen, for example, serves many functions. It is a space for cooking, eating, living, holding meetings, socialising, doing paperwork, where the kids do their homework, where you hang wet coats on the back of chairs so they'll dry by the morning. It is the hub of the home and essentials include a large table, a Belfast sink and an Aga or wood stove. A small sofa or couple of comfy armchairs go down well too. A dresser is ideal for providing a country-living look and displaying your favourite crockery, not to mention all those important receipts amongst your antique plates.

No matter how much you tidy up and yell, wellies are strewn at the back door and farming paraphernalia is left all over the house. The farmer dashes in for something and kicks off the wellies in the back hall. Bits of straw and muck fall off his trousers as he races into the kitchen, the farm dog sneaks in after him, and a farm cat slinks in the back door hoping for a tasty snack.

Grass seeds, corn or calf feed end up spread all over the bedroom floor. If you happen to get away for a few days, you may even come home to grass growing on the damp towels he left on the bathroom floor. The floors look like they need a lawn mower rather than a hoover or a mop. You consider letting the hens in like they used to do years ago – at least they might eat up all the seed and food scraps off the floor!

You may decide to forget about his and her towels – it's going to be his and her bathrooms from now on.

Your husband thinks you are wonderful if you don't shout at him for making a mess, if you don't stress about it and keep the house reasonably tidy. Your in-laws think you're perfect if you keep it spotlessly clean, as long as they don't hear you shouting at him.

Do keep all the offending articles you have found in the washing machine over the years so you can present them to your partner if he ever complains about the expense of a new washing machine.

Get two laundry baskets: one for normal clothes and one for the farm clothes. He never remembers which is which so label them.

A farmer is often guilty of not emptying his pockets before putting his work clothes in the laundry basket. If you, as a perfect farm wife, check the pockets before putting the clothes into wash, be careful as you can stab your fingers on sharp screws or fence staples.

How to use traditional cleaning materials

The best cleaning materials are hot water, soap and elbow grease. We're lucky, we can turn on a tap and hot water flows out. By 1946, 92% of urban homes had piped water and 35% had a fixed bath. In comparison, only 9% of rural homes had piped water and 4% had a fixed bath.[34] The only way to have a bath was to carry in buckets of water, heat the water on a stove, fill up a tin bath and then empty it afterwards. Only 12% of rural houses had piped water by 1960, even though the Department of Agriculture offered a 50% grant towards the cost of a water pump from 1954.

The ICA stated no woman would marry a farmer if the farmhouse didn't have running water. They were appalled that brides were being asked to "love, honour and carry water". As there was concern over the number of bachelor farmers then, I presume they thought it was an effective threat. Indeed, some women held out and insisted, although it was the 1970s before most houses had bathrooms installed.

The Irish Press 23 Oct 1947

The small farmer's wife is a miracle. And this morning our late hostess is feeding corn to her pullets in the sloping field that is one side of a valley Turner missed.

The woman of the house works day in and out in a big stone-floored kitchen. "How awful," think some, and "how tiring." But this is not true, the truth is that the springiness has stayed, where nature put in, in the arch of her foot and not in floorboards or in rugs.

If we must do something for her, she would appreciate running water near the door where the men might wash their boots, and she would appreciate warm water where they could wash their hands without calling for a kettle.

What she does not long for is a planned kitchen with a lot of town house "amenities" that require washing or polishing, for she is already cook, washerwoman, nurse and caterer, often on a big scale.

She is the needlewoman, in her spare time she lends a hand with the milking and all the time she feeds the fowl and the pigs.

Twice a week she churns or carries out a big basket of eggs on a rickety lane, whatever the weather.

She is the wife of a small farmer or is she a miracle?

Please give her water laid on and give her electricity and wish her luck. She has much to contend with but at least she is spared the fate of the house-proud townswoman who spends her time "keeping up with the Joneses" and who dusts and polishes and tidies so much that she must occasionally wonder why she was not born complete with polishing pads on her palms and suction cleaner equipment somewhere else!

This piece from 1947 celebrates the amount of work a farm woman achieves and begs for piped water to ease her workload. It sees her work as purposeful compared to the endless cleaning of women living in towns. Yes, this writer views endless cleaning and dusting as fanciful and a waste of time. Thank goodness for all that hard work – it means she can bring in an income and saves her having to compete with her neighbours on cleanliness.

The arguments continued for another two decades with the ICA launching a "Turn on the Tap" exhibition in the early 1960s and many newspapers echoing the senselessness of carrying water when the technology was there for it to be piped.

The Kerryman 30 May 1959

It is not a luxury to have running water in your kitchen, it is just plain common sense. Think of the time you waste and the energy you use up in carrying buckets of water. Then think of the comfort that plenty of water for washing, cooking and laundry would bring to your home.

Why were rural homes so slow to get piped water considering the existence of the grant and the arguments presented in various newspapers?

The National Farmers Association argued that piped water would increase the rate charges so farmers followed that lead. After all, they had wives and children to lug the water for free! Before a rural woman could start her cleaning, she had to carry the water in buckets, light the fire and heat the water. She couldn't even have a cup of tea without the bucket of water and the fire. Many young brides were even accused of being lazy by their mothers-in-law when they managed to install piped water in the house. No wonder my mother created quite a stir when she got a dishwasher in the late 1960s.

Before you start to think we're lazy nowadays with our hot water, electric washing machines and dishwashers, remember they didn't have electric light so the dust wasn't too obvious. I heard of a woman who, on getting electricity for the first time, immediately switched the lights off again as so many cobwebs came into view. Electric light and large windows mean houses have to be cleaner!

We have the hot water. We also have chemical cleaners, but are they safe to use? Are the older, tried and tested, cleaning methods more effective? Household cleaning agents aren't particularly good for your health or the environment, have a strong scent and can be expensive. Using the old-fashioned and time-tested methods to clean your house will leave it sparkling and you can enjoy a smug feeling of satisfaction. You won't fail to impress your mother-in-law either. You'll also cut down on your household shopping bills leaving all the more money to spend on milk chocolate. You have to support the dairy farmers after all.

How to use bicarbonate of soda

A competent farm wife will always have a supply of bread soda/bicarbonate of soda (same product but called by both names) in the house. Apart from being an important ingredient in traditional soda bread, you can use it to eliminate smells. If the farm dog dares enter the house and leaves a damp smell, sprinkle soda on your rugs or carpets and hoover it up. Use it in the same way if milk is spilt on upholstery or carpets.

To get rid of any stubborn or burnt food on the cooker hob, mix half a cup of bicarbonate with enough hot water to form a paste, spread it on the hardened food and leave it for a while before wiping off with a damp cloth. The same goes for cleaning the oven or any stubborn stains on the worktop. If they are very stubborn, it takes a few goes! Use a paste to clean stainless steel taps and sinks.

Bicarbonate of soda is an essential ingredient in animal cures too. Calves become bloated if they are greedy and eat too much meal. A dose of bicarbonate helps to reduce the acidity in the stomach, although you also have to run them around the calf shed numerous times! Yes, it always happens at night and you really did feel like a mini workout at 11pm, didn't you?

And if you end up with indigestion after all this cleaning and exercise, you can knock back a spoonful yourself. It might be handy to have a glass of wine in the other hand.

How to clean with lemons

You don't have to buy lemons especially for cleaning but if you've used the juice from a lemon in a fruit salad or sliced one for your G&T in the evening (did I hear you say "chance would be a fine thing"?) or have some left over from making lemonade or elderflower cordial, use the rest of the lemon in the following ways.

- Place half a lemon in your dishwasher for a wash (you need to skewer it onto one of the plate racks or into the cutlery tray) and both the dishwasher and the dishes will smell fresh. It also gets rid of any dried water marks.

- Leaving half a lemon in the fridge makes it smell fresh.

- Clean your microwave easily with half a lemon by squeezing some lemon juice into water in a jug, adding some rind and heating for a few minutes. Let it stand for five minutes and the steam will loosen those stubborn food splatters. They should be easy to wipe away and the lemon will make it smell fresh.

- To clean a wooden chopping board or a butcher's block, sprinkle the surface with coarse salt and then rub with the juice side of a half lemon. Leave for five minutes and scrape off the liquid; then wash or wipe down with warm water.

How to clean with vinegar

Vinegar is excellent for cleaning. For washing windows put a generous splash of vinegar into the water and it gives them a good shine. If they just need a quick rub over, use a vinegar and water mix in a spray bottle and rub dry with kitchen towel or newspaper. If the house is near the farmyard, enforce a speed limit of farm machinery to keep down the dust and keep the windows clean. If only a restraint could be put on the birds too!

Admittedly a window cleaner coming round every few weeks would be even handier. If the farmer baulks at the cost of getting a decorator in and says he will do it himself, he will certainly be lifting you up in the digger bucket to wash the upstairs windows rather than pay for a window cleaner.

Vinegar is also an essential ingredient for your food cupboard – after all, you're going to need it for pickling the shallots and beetroot growing in the garden and for making salad dressings for your own lettuce and salad leaves. Once you've overdosed on salads, you can sprinkle some on your chips.

How to get rid of stains

Living on a farm means that you end up with the most dubious of marks on clothing. Mix 400ml of white vinegar with 2 teaspoons of bicarbonate, stir until it stops fizzing and then put into a bottle to squirt on any stains on clothes. If you want to shift stains on white clothes, add the juice of half a lemon.

Years ago, the wives of "strong" farmers (those with thirty acres or more) had a front parlour for entertaining important visitors such as the local priest. The parlour was a status symbol, the best furniture and china were on display and it was always kept tidy and pristine should any visitors call unexpectedly. When building your own house, don't think to yourself "oh, we don't need a good sitting room; we'll hardly ever use it". That's the point. It is a room that is protected from the rigours of farm dust, the farmer, the children and their toys. Unless you make the mistake of using it as a handy store room, it should be in an acceptable state to usher visitors into.

Make a few things easier for yourself in the cleaning department. If you get gifts of decorative silver, exchange them for pewter. Do you know why? When exposed to air, silver tarnishes and so needs regular polishing. Pewter and bronze will actually lose some of their patination if you polish them so they just need a quick dust. Much easier than polishing silver.

I heard of a farmer's wife washing the kitchen floor half a dozen times a day and how the farmer walking in wearing his boots used to infuriate her. You can either threaten him with the carving knife for not leaving his boots in the back hall or let him step on cut-offs of fabric and slide across the floor, thereby keeping dirt on the fabric and polishing your floor at the same time. Of course, it is a health and safety risk as there is a risk he might slip and fall over but then he should have known to take his boots off!

How to dry clothes using a clothes line

We have it pretty easy now, although we wash clothes more frequently than they did in the past. We just pop a load of clothes (white, colours or farming clothes) into the washing machine and can choose whether to dry them on a clothes line or in the tumble dryer. We don't have to do all the washing in one day but can spread it out over the week, targeting the sunniest days so we can hang it on the line. We don't have to hang surplus clothes on hedges or drape them around the kitchen.

As we all know, clothes dried outside smell fresher. Plus you will be gaining perfect-farm-wife points if the neighbours see your line regularly filled, *so long as* you don't leave it out longer than necessary.

A perfect farm wife won't waste electricity by drying garments in the dryer (although finishing them off to save ironing is fine). Here in Ireland, despite the country's likelihood of rain, most farm wives do their utmost to get clothes hung out in the fresh air. We hang them out between the showers and regard those who use dryers in good-weather countries as almost sinful. Your ability to tell a "good drying day" will mark you out as a perfect farm wife, as will predicting what the clouds will do and running at high speed to whip dry clothes off the line as drops start to fall.

Rotary lines are good but a long clothes line allows towels, sheets and shirts to blow with wild abandon. Some people bring in the clothes pegs after every use as they will rust or perish if left outside. (Others think life is too short and leave them on the line.)

If you leave clothes out overnight and they are visible to neighbours or in-laws, they are bound to be talked about. I remember visiting a friend and she was wondering why her neighbours were so silly to hang out their clothes in the evening, but I had the answer as I did that frequently too. Our tiny urban back garden faced east so early rays of the sun had a chance to dry them, as long as it didn't rain overnight of course. Country gardens are large enough to have sunshine from all angles so country neighbours don't see the sense in that. Plus there might be more birds about!

There's an art to hanging out washing:

- ☙ To make it look orderly, hang the same items together: trousers with trousers, shirts with shirts.

- ☙ A rotary line is ideal for hiding your underwear behind the towels and preserving your dignity, but they are not so good for drying in general. If you have the room, a long clothes line is best, although three parallel lines are needed if you want to hide your underwear from prying eyes.

- ☙ Hang trousers by the waist so you don't have to iron out the peg marks on the trouser legs.

- ☙ Watch for rain clouds so you can retrieve the laundry at a moment's notice. That's the real test in Ireland!

- ☙ Bring it in by the early evening or it will become damp with the moistness from the dew. If there is a rookery nearby, there's a risk of bird dirt from the crows doing their evening circling ritual too.

There are more dangers than rain to ruining the drying process. Hanging clothes out when the farmer is agitating (stirring) slurry or spreading dung means that the pong hangs heavy on the air. "Eau de Slur-ray" infiltrates every pore of the wet clothes so they retain the odour until they are washed again! Not exactly the fragrant smell of a fabric softener!

Before you start to complain about this clothes drying malarkey being a lot of work, spare a thought for the farm women who had to hand wash clothes and bedding. They had to heat the water, wash the clothes using their bare hands and a washboard, wring them out in a mangle (Brian's maternal grandmother fattened piglets one year so she could buy a spinner to make life easier), get them dry and then look forward to ironing them the next day using a couple of heavy irons heated at the fire. Hanging out that load of clothes doesn't look such hard work now does it?

If you want to boast about getting your clothes dry outside all year round, put a clothes line in an airy hay shed too. The roof will keep the rain off and the wind will blow them reasonably dry. Watch out for roosting pigeons though!

How to catch a mouse

Animals on the farm aren't all cute and cuddly. Living on a farm means vermin can be prevalent. Farm cats can keep the rat population down: feed them enough to keep them around but not so much that they won't hunt for rats! There's a risk of mice and rats getting into the house when the nights first turn cold in early winter. You need to be vigilant if you don't want to share your home with these creatures.

Some people put down humane traps and release the mouse back into the wild. I'm of the opinion that if they dare enter my house, they dice with death. If you have the same attitude but can't bear to touch the trap when there's a dead mouse in it, either get your perfect farm husband to do it or lift both trap and mouse with the coal shovel and throw both into the fire.

I am terrified of mice. Don't even mention rats. I would prefer to face a bull any day. Just before we went on holidays last winter, we could hear the rustling of a mouse (or maybe mice) in the attic and under the floorboards in our bedroom. Brian put down a trap but no success. More action was required so before we headed off on holidays, we placed four traps around the house, and left poison in our bedroom and the attic.

I was convinced there would be four dead mice there when we got home and dreaded walking upstairs, but all traps were untouched. The poison in the attic had been disturbed but there weren't any little bodies to be seen. The poison in our bedroom hadn't been touched. I hoped we were now mouse-free but left the traps there to be on the safe side.

We could still hear the scratching of a mouse under the floorboards occasionally. It terrified me – what if it came up into the bedroom? Then one morning, I could hear a really loud clicking and scratching sound. The room was pitch black. I lay there hardly breathing. It sounded like something was near the window. "Brian," I stage-whispered, "are you awake?" (don't hesitate about waking your farm husband from a deep sleep if concerned about such a terrifying emergency) "I can hear the mouse, can you?"

"It's me doing the alarm, you eejit," he said, and I realised that he was about to get up and the clicks were the re-setting of the alarm clock for me. Phew! We never heard the mouse again so he either headed back outside as the weather got warmer or met a dismal end.

 Delegate responsibility to the farmer for getting rid of the mice. After all, he is accustomed to dealing with any vermin outside too.

How to catch a bird or a bat

Occasionally a bird or a bat might appear in one of your rooms, having come down the chimney or through an open window. Be careful as bats are a protected species, besides which you don't want a death on your conscience. (Such compassion needn't extend to mice – see above.)

Shut the door so it won't go into other rooms and open the windows wide. Leave the room as quickly as possible and hope it will fly out the window. If not, you might have to trap it in a large towel and transport it gently outside to be released.

 This is another one to delegate. If no one's around, just shut the door and hope it flies out through the window.

How to be environmentally friendly

There is a Sod's Law in farming. If you ever throw anything away, the farmer looks for it within days! Recycling is fashionable now but it has always been a way of life on farms. If your friends get fed up of you talking about the farm, change the topic to upcycling or recycling so everyone can get involved. You'll beat them hands down – every farm wife worth her salt must know how to be environmentally friendly, and it is not just about having a windmill or solar power.

As people are becoming more eco aware, reducing our carbon footprint is important in the production and distribution of food. Dairy and suckler farmers can determine their individual carbon footprint for producing food, partly thanks to helpful scientists calculating the environmental effects of gases produced by bovines. Mind you, much of the problem is the distance the product travels from production to consumption. Has the beef or lamb you are eating travelled far? Of course not – it went from the farm to the abattoir and back to your freezer.

Top tips for recycling:

🐾 Have a welly wall. Once a welly gets a hole in it, punch a few holes in the bottom for drainage, fix to the wall with a couple of screws or nails, fill with compost and plant your herbs. If there was ever a reason to buy colourful wellies, this is it.

🐾 Never throw away or recycle both wellies if one gets a hole. Put the holey one on your welly wall and keep the other in case it matches the unholey one next time a welly springs a leak. Wearing odd wellies is fine; they'll be splattered with muck most of the time anyway. If others laugh, they are obviously less caring for the environment.

🐞 Where would you be without those blue or orange bits of baler twine? Once the baler twine comes off the straw or hay bales, it has another life (or two) ahead of it. Use it to repair fences, secure temporary electric wire fences, repair halters, replace a belt in trousers, repair a clothes line, act as a lead for the dog, tie the navel cord of a newborn calf if it is bleeding, tie the tops of bags of meal, tie gates, twist to make firelighters ... the list is endless. In fact, a farmer without twine in his pockets might be viewed as a strange character (just don't forget to remove it for the washing machine).

🐞 If you want to keep weeds down around newly planted trees or in your strawberry patch, use large cardboard boxes or old carpet (made from natural fibres). We dug up the strawberry patch this year, put down an old carpet (pattern side down), made small holes and replanted the strawberry plants. It has really reduced the weeds. The cardboard and carpet dies away in time ... dust to dust.

🐞 A competent farm wife reuses rather than recycles newspaper. Scrunch up sheets to dry the freshly washed windows. (Wear gloves if you don't want to end up with black hands from the newsprint.) If you have a woodstove, dampen the newspaper slightly and dip into the cool ash; rub it over the glass to remove the soot and smoke and the glass will sparkle. Scrunch newspaper pages tightly for lighting the fire. Put under the hens' roost to make cleaning the hen shed easier – then put the paper on the compost heap. Put on the floor for muddy wellies, and use for all manner of cleaning up jobs. Broadsheets are so much better than tabloid for all these uses by the way!

🐞 When the cows are dry (they have a couple of months' rest from milking before calving), buy your milk in plastic containers and keep them to store colostrum when cows start calving. It is needed if some cows don't have enough for their own calves. Use a different type of container when freezing elderflower cordial in case they get mixed up and you don't realise until it has defrosted!

🫖 A perfect farm wife doesn't need to bring empty jars to the recycling centre. She won't be buying many either as she'll be making her own preserves. You can recycle them for your homemade jams, marmalade and chutneys.

🫖 Much is written about the volume of food waste in households. Most leftovers in a farm household can be eaten by animals. Dogs love leftover dinners of meat, potatoes and gravy; farm cats like a nibble at them too. Your few hens will love cooked vegetable peelings, leftover vegetables and pasta. You can recycle the hens' eggshells too, by drying them out in the oven (when it is cooling down after cooking your roast), crushing them and mixing them in their feed.

🫖 Grass cuttings from your lawn can be eaten by livestock or you can fence off part of the garden and let a couple of steers, sheep or donkeys be the lawnmowers. (Never give grass cuttings to donkeys or horses, as it can kill them.)

🫖 Jeans and shirts that become worn or unfashionable can be demoted to farm clothes. Use old pillowcases and torn T-shirts as cleaning rags and tear old sheets to make bandages for emergencies.

🫖 Pallets have a multitude of uses. They can be used as fencing, blockades, repairs for the hen house, and can even be used for putting pots on when hung on the wall, or turned into garden furniture (if anyone has to time to actually make it).

Don't forget to check out our "Farm Recycling" page on the website for even more ideas – see www.irishfarmerette.com. Feel free to add your own ideas and photographs too.

Have a number of bins for the different recycling items or your utility will look somewhat disorderly.

How to train a farmer to do housework

Depending on your husband's natural aptitude for cleaning and cooking or how well he was trained by his mother, you might find he needs very clear instructions. If you ask him to wash the floor, he will do exactly that – he might not realise he has to sweep it first. He might also forget to throw away the water and leave the mop and bucket inside the back door for you to fall over when you return with the shopping. Just like you would explain to a child, break the task down into little jobs so they all get done.

Whether a farmer does housework or not can depend on how busy you both are. Divide the housework if you are working off farm or in a farm-related business, although cut him some slack when he's working all hours during the calving or harvesting. If you're both running the farm and sharing the childcare, I bet you do most of the housework. If you're happy with that, that's fine – just don't fall into the trap of thinking "I might as well do it myself and do it properly".

What became apparent when chatting to farm wives was most did all the housework when they first got married. As the novelty wore off and children arrived, they found that getting their partners to do some household chores meant that he expected less and appreciated more.

DOMESTIC GODDESS

Just as an army marches on its stomach, farmers need good food for long days of physical work. Bachelors often lived (and possibly still do) on a diet of potatoes with bacon for dinner while tea was bread with jam. A woman on the farm made all the difference when it came to cooking.

Monica Sheridan, Ireland's First Celebrity Chef and winner of the Jacobs TV Personality Award 1965
"Another essential to good cooking is a husband or son with an adventurous palate. Women do not cook for other women or for themselves. If they are cooking for other women it is to annoy them or dazzle them."

".... the longevity of rural men and women could be put down to porridge, wholemeal bread, Irish stew and refusing to have anything to do with paying tax."[35]

Farm dinners have a well-deserved and long reputation of being wholesome, nutritious, meaty, large and home-cooked. Traditionally they are plates heaped with slices of meat, multiple scoops of mashed potato and at least two vegetables, all swimming in gravy. Wholesome desserts are smothered with lashings of custard or full cream. That is exactly what happens on dinner tables around the country most days of the week. Wholesome – yes; nutritious – yes; need to exercise or engage in physical activity to work it off – yes. If you're thinking that you will put on weight with this lifestyle, you might be right.

At least the regular consumption of takeaways and fast food is limited due to the distance from town to farm.

How to win a (hypothetical) Housewife of the Year prize

It's not possible to win it any more as the annual competition for "Housewife of the Year" is no more – but if it was still running, you'd be a contender once you've finished reading this book, wouldn't you?

The competition was so popular that finalists were interviewed by Gay Byrne, the *Late Late Show* presenter, and the final was broadcast on national television. Participants had to complete tasks such as design and make a garment, change a tyre, invent economic yet tasty meals for the family, and sometimes cook them to demonstrate they were a perfect housewife. They were judged on appearance, personality, overall intelligence, sense of humour, civic spirit, sincerity and their interests outside the home.

One year, applicants had to explain how they would spend £5,000 on a home or farm project (hmmm, new milking parlour or new kitchen?), design and make a summer dress for an evening party and create an original recipe for an economic meal using Irish beef or lamb.

Were the prizes worth winning? They included kitchen cabinetry, central heating installation, cookers and cash prizes. Celebrations were held in the winner's town, and she was profiled in various magazines and was a celebrity for some time.

The competition ended in 1995, apparently because too many women outside the home were taking part and winning!

Perfect farm wives, indeed, if able to bring in an income, raise a family and win a competition like that. I think I'll stick to writing about it!

How does the Housewife of the Year compare to the competitions of today? Some elements, such as creating recipes and competitive cooking, are extremely popular. You can scarcely turn on the TV without seeing professional chefs and bakers providing contenders with feedback. The finalist interview wasn't too dissimilar from the Rose of Tralee, except she had to be married (it was for house*wives* after all), have children (otherwise how could she prove her efficiency in cooking) and reveal how she looked so glamorous while cooking nutritious meals, knitting jumpers and socks for all of them and making her own clothes. (Remember that Singer sewing machine booklet I mentioned earlier?)

Nowadays, you can prove your capabilities by entering (and winning) classes in the local agricultural show. They might be easier to win, and you need concentrate on one aspect only (spend the year perfecting your scone making and no one need know your jam never sets and your knitting has dropped stitches). Read on for more tips.

How to win awards at agricultural shows

A perfect farm wife can demonstrate her talent for crafting, sewing, cooking or baking at numerous agricultural shows around the country. If you would like to master your craft, joining a local ICA or WI group will show you what the competition is like and teach you how to improve. There are so many categories you can enter – choose from brown bread, scones, cakes, vegetables, floral arranging, patchwork, crochet, quilting or photography, to name but a few.

If you are nervous about entering a show competition and dreading the stress of baking early that morning, try something you can do in advance such as jam making, baking a fruit cake, patchwork, crochet or photography.

The secret is in the preparation. Scout around this year to establish the least popular categories. If there are only three entries, the worst you can do is achieve a third place and no one else need know that third means last.

Be ready for the competitive nature of these shows. You may think it is just a bit of fun. It might be your first year but the daggers are drawn if you walk away with lots of ribbons, plus you'll have to keep the side up for all future entries.

Don't enter the "best coffee cake" competition unless you are very confident. For some reason, that class has the most entries! Having said that, if you would like to try a coffee cake recipe from olden days, here's a good one from a 1950s magazine:

Coffee cake

Coffee sponge is a very good sponge, but it must be beaten for twenty minutes, and you can't shirk that. [Lucky for us that twenty minutes by rotary mixer means five by electric beater.]

Ingredients

4 eggs
The weight of 3 eggs* in sugar
The weight of 2 eggs in flour
1 tablespoon coffee essence
Pinch salt
When I make this sponge I use white flour as I find it rises better. It is well worth the little extra expense as the amount of flour is small. [Women either ground their own or bought flour

from a mill – it's interesting that the white flour was more expensive.]

Method

Put the eggs into a bowl and beat them a little. Now add the sugar and pinch of salt and with a rotary egg beater beat for ten minutes. Add the coffee essence and beat for a further ten minutes.

Sieve the flour onto the egg mixture. Do not stir or beat. Use a large spoon and fold the flour over and over until it is mixed with the egg mixture.

Pour into two 8-inch [20-cm] sandwich tins and bake in a hot but not very hot oven for about twenty minutes. [We baked it at 180°C.] It is cooked when pressing a finger on the top leaves no depression. It will also shrink a little from the sides.

Put together with coffee filling.

*We weren't sure whether to weigh the eggs in their shells or to crack them and weigh them without shells. We asked Twitter but people differed in their opinions so we tried both ways. The weight equivalent to the eggs in shells created a lighter sponge, so go for that one.

When baking, never use eggs laid within the last three days. For best results, use eggs that are at least four days old as they make a lighter cake.

The religion of baking

Did it ever occur to you that your religion might indicate your baking abilities? Apparently, Protestants have a "baking language". While Roman Catholics were buying tins of USA biscuits in the 1970s and 1980s, Protestants were bringing "traybakes"[36] to parish functions and a "cake per car" to choral festivals and fundraisers. With this heritage of baking,

Protestants would never dream of bringing bought cakes to a parish sale or school function. It's useful to know: the religion of your future mother-in-law might give you a hint as to the challenge that lies ahead in meeting her expectations.

By the way, Methodists and Presbyterians raise the bar further. Their decorated cakes and organised freezers are a sight to behold.

How to be self-sufficient

Farm wives in the past were reputed to be frugal, and indeed that's exactly what their dearly beloved wanted – at least when it came to spending money on the household.

Meath Chronicle 10 October 1914
Servant boy (to farmer's wife noted for her thriftiness) "Well, Ma'am, my eyesight must be getting bad. I can't see the butter on the bread this morning."

Next morning the farmer's wife put the butter a little thicker on the bread, and remarked "Well, Tommy, I hope your eyes are better this morning."

"Begod, ma'am" replied Tom "they're grand this morning. I can see the bread through the butter."

Some letters to newspapers and magazines, even women's magazines, warned against wives who were extravagant or wasteful.

Woman's Way 1 June 1963
Always watch the way your sweetheart eats cheese. If she removes it wastefully or eats it without taking the rind off, she won't make a good wife, but if she takes it off economically, she's the girl for you.[37]

Whether you are trying to live the good life or just produce some of your own food, being self-sufficient to a degree can be very satisfying. Our fore-mothers did it out of necessity. They harvested potatoes. They grew carrots, turnips and parsnips. They planted onions, lettuce and broad beans. Some ground their own flour. They baked bread daily and cakes frequently. They had hens for eggs, chickens for the table and cows for milk. They made their own butter and butchered their own pig each year. While they didn't have much money to buy goods from shops, there was good food on the table. As the proverb says, a cabin with plenty of food is better than a hungry castle.

We have much easier access to food now with the convenience of supermarkets. We can source almost all our food for the week in less than an hour. However, the appreciation of producing your own food is growing. Impress friends by serving vegetables from your garden or present them with a gift of fresh eggs. It's a lovely feeling when you can cook a whole meal and almost every ingredient comes from your own vegetable garden or farm.

Start small; once you find it manageable, it is easier to grow on your successes. A couple of raised beds for easy-growing fruit and vegetables such as rhubarb, raspberries, strawberries, runner beans and beetroot will get you going. Get three or four hens too. Eggs have to be one of the easiest foods to source (you don't have to milk or slaughter the hens to get a yummy source of protein) and the providers have fun personalities, too.

How to eat your home-produced meat

I'm not referring to cooking your meat rare, medium or well done. You see, it can be difficult to eat your own slaughtered animals if you are fond of them and know their personalities.

On the other hand, there is no point sending animals to the factory and buying meat in the supermarket, and not making the real connection between them.

Kate loves lamb chops. When we had two pet lambs, Matilda and Bill, we were debating whether to slaughter Matilda for meat or let her have lambs of her own. Kate's response at four years of age was "I can't wait till Matilda is yummy in my tummy". (We did keep Matilda and she went on to have many sets of triplets.)

 Don't name the animal that is going to end up in the freezer, at least not with a "human name". Otherwise, you end up leaving it in the freezer for a long time as you acclimatise to the idea of eating Jack or Susie.

Calling them Mint Sauce, Chops, Rashers, Sausages or Sirloin might seem harsh, but it makes the meat much more appetising than wondering if it is Daisy or Frank that you are scoffing with relish.

How to prepare a chicken for the table

I'm not talking about an oven-ready chicken here, but about you rearing or purchasing chicks to produce your own meat.

If you are fed up wondering if the chickens you buy really are free-range or would like sufficiently large chickens to last your family for two days. I recommend you have a go at rearing your own (just don't give them names!). Don't buy too many all in one go – we purchased eighteen chicks once and by the time we got to the last few they were almost as big as small turkeys. While it is handier to slaughter four or six all in one go, you need to set aside plenty of time to do it.

First catch the chicken without causing stress (I mean to the chicken, not you). Creep up behind them stealthily just after giving them food and pick one up. If they are accustomed to being held occasionally, it won't mind it in the least. Hold it under your arm and pull its neck quickly to one side to wring it. Don't worry too much if the wings flap afterwards as that's normal and doesn't mean it is still alive. Alternatively, get your other half to do this deed. I always delegate it.

Pluck the bird while it is still warm; pull out the feathers in the direction in which they are lying to avoid tearing the skin. Don't be surprised if each bird takes twenty minutes.

If you'd really like to be industrious, keep feathers to use for stuffing a cushion or something similar. Duck feathers are particularly soft. Years ago, women kept the strong feathered part of the wings to use as dusters for hard-to-reach places.

Let the chicken hang in a cool place overnight or for a couple of days. To clean out the insides then, it's handy if you have a small table in your utility, covered with a washable or disposable plastic cloth. It's a case of getting your hands in there to get it all out. Some of the offal will be edible – there's many a farmer who loves chicken liver with a fry-up.

Weigh it so you can work out the cooking time or pop in a plastic bag and into the freezer. Did I mention a big chest freezer is essential?

Your own roasted free-range chicken will be the nicest you ever taste. If the thought of killing, plucking and cleaning out your own chickens and ducks is too much for you, it is possible to outsource that part to professionals.

How to set a table

In all farming households I know, dinners are almost always eaten at the kitchen table.

Some people don't know how to set a table. On being given the job of laying the table for dinner, an American visitor spent ten minutes working out where to place everything, only to have my mum rearrange it all in twenty seconds flat.

While the ideal might be an embroidered fabric tablecloth, an oilcloth that can be washed and wiped is much more sensible. Napkins can look good, but realistically sheets of kitchen paper will be handier.

Complete sets of crockery and cutlery may be the ideal of a perfect farm wife, but if you can get co-ordinating, rather than matching, ones they can still be charming. While you may have started off with matching sets, numerous breakages and loss (teaspoons never seem to make it back from the farm picnics and sharp knives tend to walk to the farmyard) mean you end up with an eclectic mix after a few years.

A table set with a knife, fork, dessert spoon and fork, and side plate for each person suggests order and will hint to the farmer that the dinner is ready, but it is also fine if you occasionally throw the required cutlery in the centre of the table and let the first person sitting down allocate them to everyone. Condiments of pepper and salt, real butter in a butter dish, full fat milk in a jug and a large jug of cold water can be placed in the centre. (I wouldn't risk skimmed milk or any of the "butter" spreads.)

It used to be widespread that the "man of the house" sat at the head of the table. In some areas years ago men and boys ate before women and daughters could sit at the table to eat their meals and were given the best cuts of meat and freshest bread. Times change and unless he is going to jump up and down to serve and make the tea, it's handier if he is out of the way at the back of the table, seating any restless child on his knee while eating.

Our son used to love eating from Brian's bowl of cornflakes while sitting on his knee at breakfast time. I think the liberal sprinkling of sugar had something to do with it.

As soon as the children are old enough, make setting the table one of their jobs.

How to cook a dinner fit for a ~~king~~ farmer

A perfect farm wife plans the meals for the week before she goes grocery shopping. This reduces waste and ensures she isn't missing a crucial ingredient in the middle of cooking a meal. The expression "fail to prepare, prepare to fail" is as pertinent for efficient planning of family meals as a business.

If you find cooking meals to be a time-consuming chore, here are some suggestions for quick, easy and tasty dinners farmers will love. Farmers are very similar to their animals: they like routine – they have their favourite meals and don't like change.

Shepherd's (lamb) or cottage (beef) pie

You can make this from raw minced meat, but I usually mince up leftovers from Sunday's roast. Cook a double amount of potatoes on the Sunday too as it saves you having to boil up fresh potatoes for the pie.

Fry chopped onion and chopped carrot in a pan until softened, add the cooked minced meat, stir in a decent spoonful of flour (or cornflour), add half a pint of beef stock (accomplished farm wives make their own, of course), and a really generous squirt of tomato ketchup or tomato puree. If you're more adventurous, you could also add a splash of Tabasco or Worcester sauce. While it is bubbling contentedly, add in a large handful of frozen peas. Turn into a large casserole dish.

Add some butter to mashed potato and spoon it on top of the meat mixture; even it out with a fork leaving little peaks that will crust when cooking. Sprinkle some grated cheese over if you want. Cook for about forty minutes at 180°C. (Thirty minutes if the farmer happens to be early, fifty if he's late.) This is a wonderfully tasty comfort dinner for cold winter days.

Roast dinner

Some farm households have a roast almost every day – be it roast beef, roast leg of lamb, lamb chops or roast chicken. It is less expensive if you get a butcher to slaughter a beef heifer and a lamb and put them in your humungous freezer.

While some people baulk at cooking a roast, it really is the easiest dinner of all as the meat doesn't seek any attention and cooks away in the oven. If you're in the house, baste it, but if you're busy outside, it will be fine. Alternatively use a roasting bag to keep all the juices around the meat (saves washing up too). Then it is just a case of cooking potatoes, one or two vegetables and making the gravy.

Farmers tend to like their meat well done which is just as well seeing they are often late in for dinner. The dog's favourite dinner is a roast dinner too, all mixed up with gravy!

If you're unsure what time the farmer will be in, a vegetable dish that keeps well and doesn't dry out is a mixture of carrot and turnip (swedes are called turnips in Ireland, by the way). Chop the turnip/swede into one-inch pieces and put on to boil. Add chopped carrot after about five minutes and simmer until they can be prodded with a fork. You can add a parsnip too for extra sweetness. Mash together, sprinkle with a little pepper and add a generous knob of butter; give it a final mash and into a covered dish in a warm oven. It stays moist for ages and is delicious.

Casseroles

The beauty of casseroles is it doesn't matter if he is a little early or really late, they still taste good. Although they take a while to cook, a casserole is very quick to prepare. It takes less than fifteen minutes to slice and chop your vegetables of carrots, onions and mushrooms and throw them into a casserole dish with the meat and liquid. You could sear the meat beforehand and use cornflour to thicken the juices, but I find an appropriate packet of casserole mix makes a very tasty casserole without doing this. If you have to use a lamb casserole mix for a chicken casserole, he won't notice the difference, I promise! Cook in the oven for approximately two hours. Make a double amount and either freeze the leftovers for a day you're in a hurry or have the rest the next day.

Omelette

Omelette and chips or omelette with mashed potato and peas is an easy and quick dinner. Fry chopped onion, mushrooms and tomato in a pan. Mix two (three for the farmer) eggs with a fork, adding in a little pepper and salt and some chopped fresh parsley (and a splash of water to make the omelette fluffier). Pour the egg mixture into a frying pan containing hot oil, and fry the omelette on a medium heat. As it is cooking, add some chopped leftover potato to the vegetable mixture and stir through to warm. Add some of the vegetable filling to the middle of the omelette once the top of the omelette is just about cooked. Flick up the omelette on each side so it folds up onto the middle and serve.

The handy thing about omelettes is you can throw the egg mixture into the pan when you see the farmer heading in. By the time he has washed his hands and had a glimpse of the newspaper or double-checked the breeding charts, it's ready.

It's not an ideal dinner if you are feeding lots of working men though – unless you have four frying pans!

Bacon and cabbage

As a traditional Irish dinner, bacon and cabbage is a firm favourite in farm households. Soak the bacon in water for twenty-four hours in case it is salty. Then place it in a large saucepan and cover with cold water; bring to the boil and let it simmer. After an hour, change the water and repeat.

Cooking times depend on the size. You can cook the cabbage in with the bacon or in a steamer above. If you want to make a quick colcannon, chop the cabbage into small pieces using a sharp knife and mix with hot mashed potato and a generous helping of butter.

Bacon and cabbage needs a good parsley sauce. Melt a generous slice of butter in a pan, add a couple of spoonfuls of flour and stir with a wooden spoon to make a roux (when it comes together in a dryish ball). Using a whisk, stir in some milk and keep whisking and adding milk until it comes to a gentle simmer. Turn it down and keep stirring until it thickens. Add in the chopped parsley. If it is too thick, just add more milk.

If the parsley sauce turns out to be lumpy because you were multi-tasking by tweeting, strain through a sieve and it will be fine. (A perfect farm wife can stir with one hand and tweet with the other, though!)

Chicken pie

This meal looks time-consuming to prepare but that's because you have to wait for the chicken mixture to cool. I'm sure you can entertain yourself by doing some paperwork, cutting the grass, hoovering the house or relaxing with a cup of tea while that is happening.

Make enough pastry for your savoury pie and a fruit tart. Even if you don't want to make the fruit tart today, leave the pastry in the fridge or freezer. Pastry is easy and quick to make but always feels like it is going to take ages so while you are making it, make plenty.

Cut chicken fillets into one-inch cubes and fry off in olive oil to seal in the juices. Add a chopped onion, two chopped garlic cloves and sliced mushrooms. Once cooked, take everything out of the saucepan and place in a bowl.

Make the sauce in the same saucepan to save on the washing up. Melt some butter, add flour to make the roux and then whisk in milk to make a sauce. Add a generous splash of chicken stock and some pepper and salt. Stir back in the chicken and vegetables and ensure all are coated. Put into the pie dish, grease the top rim and leave till cool.

Roll out the pastry and place on top. Make a couple of slits for steam to escape and bake in the oven for half an hour. Note that if you put on the pastry while the mixture is still hot, the pastry will sag and fall down into the mixture! (You can trust me on that!)

A good fry-up

A mixed grill or a fry-up can be used for breakfast, dinner or tea, but in moderation! Remember that cholesterol! Rashers, sausages, black or white pudding, leftover potatoes sliced and placed under the grill, eggy bread, fried tomatoes and fried eggs go down a treat.

It's a good idea sometimes to cook extra in case someone unexpectedly turns up for dinner – although that doesn't happen as much now as in the past. Years ago, farm women were accustomed to feeding a large crowd at dinner: husband, numerous children, workers and whatever neighbours or salesmen happened to be in the yard. Workers and large families have now diminished in number but it can still happen that someone arrives at dinner time. If you're in the habit of cooking double (so the leftovers can be frozen or eaten the following day), it's easy enough to provide an extra dinner. If your farm dog is used to getting a generous helping of leftovers all mixed with gravy, he will have to put up with dog food that day. In other words, the visitor gets the dog's dinner!

The farmer never panics about being late for dinner as he knows that you, being the accomplished farm wife, will keep his dinner perfectly hot and moist by placing the dinner plate (with another plate over the top) over a saucepan of simmering hot water. On the other hand, if he has to wait more than five minutes for his dinner when you said it would be ready, every second counts. You can delude him by having the table set so it looks like dinner is ready to be served, pass him the farming paper and he won't notice ten minutes passing.

Desserts

Desserts can be more time-consuming to make than the main course, so here are some ideas for tasty, wholesome desserts which are quick to prepare. Remember farmers are apparently experiencing heart attacks in alarming numbers so limit the creamy and chocolatey desserts to the weekends!

Rice pudding

Made with your own farm's milk, this will be a really creamy dessert. While you have to be there in case it boils over, it needs very little attention (so feel free to go on Twitter).

Put the rice with a few spoonfuls of sugar into the saucepan and add the milk. If it becomes too thick, just add more milk. Bring to an almost boil and then turn it down, stirring occasionally. If it boils over onto the hob, it makes a horrendous mess (but you'll have bicarbonate of soda at hand to help out!).

Alternatively, if you want to make it and leave it, bake it in the oven.

Rhubarb tart

Remember I said to make a double amount of pastry for the chicken pie? Leave the pastry in the fridge overnight and harvest some rhubarb from the garden. Roll out the pastry and use it to line a greased pie dish; pop in the sliced rhubarb and don't forget a generous sprinkling of sugar. Cover with more rolled pastry, and if you want to make it look pretty, cut shapes from the leftover pastry for decoration. Prod the pastry top with a fork so the steam can escape and pop in the oven for about thirty-five minutes at 180°C.

For variety, add some blackberries, raspberries or strawberries to the rhubarb when in season.

It's delicious served warm with cream, ice cream or custard. Blackberry and apple tarts are scrummy too.

Fruit crumbles

Crumble is quick to make as long as the butter is soft.

Ingredients
Your chosen fruit (e.g. sliced apple, rhubarb, plums)
225 g / 8 oz flour (a mixture of white and whole-wheat, with porridge oats if you wish)
85 g / 3 oz butter
85–110 g / 3–4 oz brown sugar

Method
Mix the flour and the butter together with your fingertips until the mixture looks like breadcrumbs.
Mix in the sugar.
Place the fruit in an oven-proof dish and spread the crumble mix over the top.
Cook in a preheated oven at 180°C.
Serve with cream, ice cream or custard.

Steamed pudding

This is a perfect comfort food on a cold day. It is often looked on as a pain to make but that's because the steaming takes a long time. It can steam away while you are cooking the rest of the dinner. You just have to make sure the water doesn't boil dry.

Ingredients

113 g / 4 oz flour (whole-wheat or white)

113 g / 4 oz brown sugar

113 g / 4 oz soft butter

2 teaspoons baking powder

2 large eggs

2 tablespoons golden syrup (for the calorific version) or a couple of generous handfuls of frozen fruit (for the healthier version)

Method

Make up the pudding by beating the flour, sugar, butter, baking powder and eggs together until you get a smooth mixture.

Put the syrup or fruit into the bottom of a greased pudding bowl, and cover with the pudding mixture.

Butter the back of a piece of tinfoil and fold a pleat in it (this provides more room if the mixture rises substantially). Place butter side down over the bowl and secure around the edge with twine. You can make a "handle" by using a double strand of twine and tie to the twine either side of the bowl. Yes, clean baler twine is perfect – see, that's another use for it.

Use a steamer if you have one, otherwise place an old saucer or plate in the bottom of a large saucepan, pour in about 8cm of boiling water, pop in your pudding (having the "handle" makes it easier) and steam for 90 minutes. If the water runs low, add more boiling water.

Turn out onto a plate and serve with cream, custard or ice cream.

Unless you are a bake-aholic, you won't want to be making desserts every day, so make large ones to last for two days. For variety, serve crumbles and tarts with ice cream the first day (when it is hot) and with custard the second day.

Teas

Teatime on a farm isn't just a cup of tea. It usually involves a cooked meal, (if you read Enid Blyton books as a child, it's exactly what the Famous Five enjoyed for their "high teas"). Yes, cooking again, but I did warn you that being a farm wife is a full-time job! Here are some suggestions for quick and easy meals.

- **Eggs:** Your own free-range eggs boiled, poached, scrambled, or coddled. All you need with them are fresh bread or toast, salt and butter.

- **Fry-up:** Sausages, rashers and a fried egg at the very least. Add baked beans, black or white pudding, mushrooms and French toast to make it more substantial.

- **Field mushrooms:** In August you should be able to find field mushrooms, particularly if there are "grand soft days". Warmth and showers are the perfect conditions. All you need with field mushrooms are slices of fresh thickly sliced white bread, buttered liberally, and a pinch of salt.

- **Salad:** Leftover meat from dinner time, hard-boiled eggs, coleslaw, tomatoes, salad onions, beetroot and lettuce, with fresh brown bread.

- **Pancakes:** All you need for pancakes are flour and your own supply of milk and eggs. Create variety by serving with different toppings such as maple syrup, lemon and sugar, butter and sugar, marmalade, Nutella, Nutella and banana or Nutella and strawberries. Or have savoury pancakes with mushrooms, onions and cheese; ham, egg and cheese, or any filling you fancy.

- **Homemade scones:** As tea (with cream and jam), or after tea. Or savoury scones with cheese.

Farmers burn a lot of energy and they like their sweet treats. You'll also find a steady flow of callers and visitors, not to mention your own family, can get through an incredible amount of your home baking. Don't presume that two dozen queen cakes will last a few days. Even in a family of four, they might last only twenty-four hours.

Some baked items, such as an egg sponge, taste much better if eaten on the day it is cooked. A family of four can get through an entire cake in two sittings – I can vouch for that. Madeira cakes, queen cakes, scones, brown bread and fruit tarts all last for a couple of days in an airtight tin. Fruit cakes or tea bracks will last longer, so are a good bake to have on hand.

The baking essentials to keep stocked up are flour, sugar, butter, cocoa, chocolate, cream, raisins, milk and eggs.

If you are the kind of person who burns everything, find a recipe that doesn't need to be baked, such as biscuit cake or trifle.

Another method of cheating takes a bit longer to come to fruition. Having a daughter (or son) who loves to bake and will do the baking for you is a tried and tested method that I have perfected! I have no idea why I am so lucky but I can heartily recommend it as the best method ever. There are no guarantees they will clean up after themselves, but you can't have it every way.

More recipes

Kate's brown bread

Ingredients

310 g / 11 oz plain white flour
140 g / 5 oz wholemeal flour
1 level teaspoon bread soda
A pinch of salt
300 ml / ½ pint buttermilk to mix (If you don't have buttermilk, use sour milk. If you don't have sour milk, add the juice of a half lemon or a teaspoon of vinegar to ordinary milk and leave it for ten minutes before using – see, no excuses!)

Method

Put the plain flour, wholemeal flour, salt and bread soda into a bowl. Mix together with a broad knife.

Add the buttermilk slowly, mixing all the time. Add enough to make a wet dough (so it looks like porridge).

Spoon the mixture into a greased and lined 1 lb loaf tin. Sprinkle a little flour on top and with a floured knife cut a line straight down the middle about a centimetre deep.

Bake in a preheated oven at 190°C for about forty minutes. When you tap the bottom, it should sound hollow.

Remove from the oven and wrap in a clean tea towel* until cool although it is extra delicious when served slightly warm with real butter.

* Don't use a tea towel that has been through the washing machine with fabric conditioner, as this will transfer to the bread and make it taste funny.

Scones / Spot o' dick

My mum always gets lots of compliments for her scones and this is her recipe. Kate has mastered the art of making perfectly light scones every time, even winning first prize with them in the local country show. The same recipe can be used to make spot o' dick, which is a homemade yeast-free fruit bread.

Both are delicious served warm with slices (yes, slices) of butter slathered over them. They are perfect for good hearty teas or picnics to the field. Eat within a day or two of making to have them at their best. Don't worry, they'll disappear all right.

Some people pronounce it skon, others say skone – it's the taste that counts!

Ingredients

455 g / 1 lb plain flour

85 g / 3 oz margarine or butter (butter is better for you)

2 teaspoons cream of tartar

85 g / 3 oz sugar

1 teaspoon bread soda*

1 egg

About 300 ml / ½ pint buttermilk (the quantity can vary according to the temperature of the room and the soakage of the flour – the more you make the scones, the easier you will find it to gauge)

(110 g / 4 oz sultanas or raisins if making fruit scones)

* Never give a full bag of bread soda to the farmer for a bloated calf; make sure to keep some in the house for your scones.

Method

Mix all the dry ingredients together (except the fruit).

Add the butter cut into cubes and mix in with your fingertips until it looks like breadcrumbs. If the butter is at room temperature and soft, it makes it much easier.

Add the fruit now if you're using it.

Add in the beaten egg.

Pour in some buttermilk a little at a time and mix with a broad knife until it all comes together. It should look like a dough but not be too wet.

Turn onto your floured table and flatten it out so it is about an inch deep.

Use a plain or serrated scone cutter to cut into rounds. (Farmers like big scones! Use a smaller cutter if they're for visitors.)

Brush a little milk on top and sprinkle on a little sugar – this will make them glisten and shine.

Bake on a baking tray at 200°C for approximately twenty minutes.

Spot o' dick

The same recipe as for the scones.

Bring the whole mixture together into a round shape (not flattened, as you would for scones) and make a vertical and a horizontal slash through the centre for a cross. Place on a floured baking tin and bake at 180° for forty minutes.

Raspberry jam

Raspberry jam is one of the easiest jams to make.

Ingredients
900 g / 2 lb sugar
900 g / 2 lb fresh raspberries
4 or 5 clean glass jars

Method
Grease the bottom of a large saucepan with butter and pour in the raspberries. Put them on hob at a low heat. At no point should you stir the fruit.

Put the sugar into a bowl and pop into a low oven to warm with the five clean jars. Putting the jars into the oven sterilises them; plus, if they are cold when you pour the hot jam in, they will crack.

Put two saucers or small plates into the freezer.

When the raspberries turn mushy (after about 10 minutes) gently fold in the warmed sugar. When the sugar has dissolved, bring it to the boil for 10 minutes. A froth will appear on the top.

Take a chilled plate out of the freezer and put a teaspoon of the jam on it, spreading it out a little. Leave it for 30 seconds and run your finger lightly over the top. If a skin has formed, it will wrinkle, which means it is ready. If not, boil for another minute and try a sample on the other chilled plate. If the froth is still in the saucepan, put in a teaspoon of butter and mix.

Once the fruit is cooked to form a skin on the sample, pour the hot jam into the warmed jam jars. Leave to cool before sealing with your jam pot covers.

Barmbrack

If you think making cakes is time-consuming, spare a thought for the women who had to spend an hour beating the mixture! Here's a recipe from a 1950s magazine and I assure you, not only is it tasty but there's plenty of eating in it! The details in brackets are our discoveries after experimenting with the recipe (as some details were a little vague!).

> Though the barmbrack is a traditional Irish and Scottish Hallowe'en cake, very few city folk now attempt to make it themselves. The following recipe is simple and reliable and makes a good-sized brack.

Ingredients

450 g / 1 lb flour (plain white)
70 g / 2.5 oz sugar
300 ml / ½ pint tepid milk
225 g / ½ lb sultanas
60 g / 2 oz mixed peel
60 g / 2 oz butter
23 g / ¾ oz yeast (dried)
1 egg
1 teaspoon salt

Method

Sieve the flour and salt into a bowl which has been warmed but has not been allowed to get hot.

Rub in the butter. Add the sugar.

Mix the yeast with 2 tablespoons of the tepid milk. Pour it into the centre of the flour, together with the beaten egg and sufficient of the tepid milk to make a stiff batter. [I usually have a tablespoon of the milk left from the amount in the ingredients, but you may have to use all of it.]

Add the fruit and beat the mixture for ten minutes with a wooden spoon until it is smooth and elastic.

Add a ring or a coin wrapped in tinfoil. [Whoever gets the ring will be next to marry or whoever gets the coin will be rich.]

Turn the mixture into a warm, greased tin, cover with a cloth and stand in a warm place to rise to double the size. [We used an 8-inch/20-cm tin with high sides. Make sure to warm it before adding the mixture – it makes a huge difference.] This will take about an hour.

Bake in a hot oven [220°C] for five minutes; reduce the heat [to 140°C] and cook for three-quarters of an hour.

Meanwhile, make a syrup to glaze the brack, as follows: Put three teaspoons of sugar and three dessertspoons of water into a small saucepan. Heat slowly until the sugar is melted. At the end of the cooking time above, paint the syrup on the brack and pop it back into the oven for a couple of minutes to dry.

Cool on a wire rack.

One-egg cake

This recipe was taken from a 1950s magazine and highlights the shortage of eggs. Even though farmers' wives probably had a plentiful supply, they sold most of them. Prices increased in the winter as supplies of eggs dropped.

Ingredients

225 g / ½ lb flour
85 g / 3 oz butter
225 g / ½ lb mixed fruit
½ teaspoon bread soda
85 g / 3 oz sugar
1 tablespoon marmalade
1 small egg, well beaten
½ cup sour milk [or ordinary milk mixed with the juice of ½ a lemon]

> This recipe dates from the middle-war years when there was no mixed peel to be had and marmalade was substituted. I still use the marmalade because it helps to sweeten the cake and darkens the colour slightly.

Method

Line and grease a medium-sized tin [We use an 8-inch/20-cm tin.]
Sift the flour into a bowl.
Cut and rub in the butter.
Add the bread soda, sugar and fruit.
Add the marmalade, the beaten egg and enough sour milk to mix to a stiff dough. Beat well.
Put into the prepared tin and bake for 75–90 minutes in a moderate oven [160°C].

Chocolate Swiss roll

This is taken from an early 1970s cook book – when they had introduced electric mixers!

Ingredients

3 eggs
140 g / 5 oz castor sugar
113 g / 4 oz plain flour
27 g / 1 oz chocolate powder [Use cocoa powder, not drinking chocolate.]
1 rounded teaspoonful of baking powder
½ teaspoon vanilla essence
Butter icing for the filling [We use whipped cream.]

Method

Beat the eggs for five minutes.

Add the sugar and beat for a further five minutes.

Fold in the sifted flour, baking powder, cocoa powder and vanilla essence.

Pour into a shallow tin, which is greased and lined.

Bake in a hot oven for 7–11 minutes. [We bake it at 190°C.]

Turn out onto sugared paper placed over a damp cloth. [We cut the edges off the long sides as it leaves a neater edge when rolled. Plus they make a great treat for the cook!]

Roll up and leave wrapped in the paper.

When the cake is cold, unroll it and spread with butter icing or whipped cream, and roll again.

How to feed contractors

Feeding contractors (the people who come to harvest silage, spread slurry or harvest crops) is common in many farming areas, although it is dying out on some farms. It is a throwback to the days when neighbouring farm families helped each other at harvest time. The host family always fed all the helpers and it was a matter of pride to provide good hospitality. Never could a neighbour leave without being fed or the host family would be most upset.

Although contractors are now employed to do the harvest, the tradition of hospitality remains. For many, providing a good meal is still a matter of pride as the word does get out as to which farming household provides the best grub. No pressure on you at all!

One advantage to feeding them is you can to some extent control when they stop for food. If rain is imminent, you can delay the dinner or tea until it actually is raining and they can't work. Coming in for a meal is probably going to take less time than if they disappear for an hour to get food too.

What do you cook them for dinner? Some households provide roast dinners followed by home-baked rhubarb or apple tarts. While this may sound relatively easy, the problem is you don't necessarily know which day they are going to arrive. If you take a joint out of the freezer to defrost and if they don't come for a few days more, you'll be eating roast beef and cottage pies for a week. Plans change, equipment breaks down, someone's ill. It can be tricky to get it right.

Nor is it easy to get men to arrive in for dinner at a precise time, although I have heard of women who strike the fear of God in them so they leave the field and file in at the appointed time. I haven't mastered that yet. If you fail at that too, you have the challenge of preventing the roast beef becoming like dried-out leather, although my mother got over that problem by keeping the dinners warm in a hostess trolley. She did offer me the hostess trolley when I took over her role, but for me, the chore of carving roasts was going a step too far.

I take an easier option. I go back to the one-pot dinner – well, two: one for potatoes and one for the casserole. Putting chopped meat and vegetables into a pot to simmer slowly for a few hours is pretty easy, you really can't go wrong. As long as you have the right type of floury potato, you are home and dry as far as gratitude from hungry farmers is concerned.

By the way, contractors aren't overly keen on vegetables such as carrots and mushrooms, so just add sufficient vegetables for colour. A bag of frozen peas cooked will meet with more approval than fresh vegetables.

Nor do they like fresh fruit from the garden, even when served with ice cream. They need the sweetness of the crumble mixture over the fruit!

Other options for dessert include rhubarb crumble, baked rice pudding and tarts made with ready-made pastry; the frozen strudels available in supermarkets go down well, too.

Silage contractors tend to be hungry and tired when they finish up late at night, and are appreciative of food and time to wind down. Cooking a fry-up at midnight mightn't be your idea of a late night snack but they'll enjoy it. It's quicker than making pans of sandwiches. If you prefer to give them sandwiches, let them make them themselves – put all the salad in the middle of the table with plenty of bread and they'll work away.

If the silage men are departing at a meal time, it is considered good farm etiquette to feed them before they leave. Otherwise, you might be viewed as an inconsiderate neighbour! After all, they might be going on to a farm where they won't be fed until they have done yet more work.

How to create a meal from almost nothing

Although a perfect farm wife should always have a fully stocked fridge, it is not always easy to achieve this when you live miles from the nearest supermarket or even from a local shop. You might be planning on cooking pancakes for tea as your cupboard is bare apart from flour, butter and sugar (along with your supply of milk) and then you get the news that there are extra mouths to be fed in the shape of a few hungry contractors. The trick is knowing how to create a hearty meal from your scanty ingredients.

As long as you have a couple of onions, a packet of rashers and perhaps some leftover potatoes, those pancakes can become omelettes. Cook potato wedges as an accompaniment by slicing raw potatoes, putting them onto a hot baking tray with a little oil and shaking chilli flakes, salt and pepper over them, and then put them into the oven at 200°C.

 There are a few essentials that you need to keep in stock or produce them from your own farm so they are always available – flour, butter, an onion or two, rashers, milk from your own cows or goats, eggs from your own hens. With these ingredients, it is possible to whip up a tea no matter who walks in the door.

How to create your signature dish

If you are aspiring to perfect farm wife status, you need to find, establish and secure your own signature dish. Every respected contributor to parish functions has at least one dish that is tasty, quick to make and yet looks sophisticated. You may think you need to vary your contributions occasionally but if you have one creation that impresses random callers, is suitable to bring to parish or school functions and is enjoyed by the extended family, it will save you a lot of time and angst. You know it is a signature bake if they all request it. Every perfect farm wife is known by her signature dish and once you see a table of bakes at a parish event, you'll know who is there before you.

My signature dish is my biscuit cake, I may be biased but I do think it is nicer than most others out there. It's always popular with children and adults. It can be made in fifteen minutes, you can keep young children occupied by getting them to break the biscuits and it freezes well. What more could you ask for?

Biscuit cake

This is perfect for farm picnics, for hungry contractors and for bringing to parish or school functions. It freezes well, it slices easily and it is deliciously chocolatey.

One word of warning: as this isn't baked and it contains egg, I always have the mixture pretty hot when adding the egg so it cooks.

Ingredients
255 g / 9 oz margarine or butter
85 g / 3 oz sugar
2 eggs
255 g / 9 oz drinking chocolate powder
300g / 1 pack of Rich Tea biscuits

I usually treble these ingredients and then cut the biscuit cake into slabs, wrap some in cling film and freeze. You may prefer to try a single batch first though.

Method

Melt the butter and sugar until the sugar is dissolved.

Break the biscuits into small pieces in a separate bowl while you are waiting (or get the children to do this).

Line a one pound tin with the butter paper so the biscuit cake will be easy to remove.

Add in the drinking chocolate, stirring well with your wooden spoon. It will thicken and become silky and glossy in appearance. It should be hot: not quite simmering, but hot. Remove from the heat.

Add the two beaten eggs immediately but a little at a time, stirring quickly. Take care to add the eggs a little at a time so they don't scramble in the heat and yet they cook.

Toss in the broken biscuits and stir to ensure they are all covered with the chocolate mixture. If you haven't broken them into small enough pieces, bash them with the wooden spoon for a few minutes. (It can be quite therapeutic!) We prefer a slightly drier biscuit cake so I add a few more biscuits than the recipe states.

Put the mixture into the tin. Pack it down as tightly as you can with the spoon, as if there are gaps (or if the biscuits are too big), the biscuit cake will crumble when it is cut.

Leave it in the fridge overnight to set. Turn out and cover with melted chocolate before slicing it.

It freezes well too so it's handy for making a triple sized one (in a big Pyrex dish) and cutting into slabs to freeze. It's not the best thing to have in the house if you're trying to lose weight.

Never try to compete with near neighbours or your mother-in-law by making the same signature dish. If you make it better, the claws will be out. You might hear something like "Hmmm, that's nice," followed by "I think your oven was a bit too hot," or "Did you sieve the flour twice? I don't think you could have done."

How to pack a picnic for the field

If you are thinking pretty polka-dot melamine tableware, a flowery rug, cucumber sandwiches and little iced fairy cakes, I'd put those out of your mind right now. Picnics for men working in the field need to be hale and hearty meals.

When my mother prepared picnic dinners for the silage contractors, this is how she did it:

- While the roast dinner and baked rice pudding were cooking, she scalded the flasks. All the mugs, cutlery, milk, cold drinks and condiments went into a box.
- She made the tea and put it into the flasks (her predecessors put tea into glass bottles, stoppered with twisted newspaper and placed in thick socks to keep them warm).
- She served up the dinners into warmed Pyrex bowls with lids, wrapped them in tea towels to keep them warm and put them into the car.
- Her dessert was usually baked rice pudding – easy to make and very filling – this was transported in an enormous bowl and ladled out there, served with lashings of thick cream.
- We wanted our farm picnic dinner too, so she had to serve up mini dinners for us as well.

The men sat around on old tyres or upturned buckets. There were no rugs. Our bare legs were scratched by the spiky grass, cut short by the mower blades.

Once they finished their mugs of tea and had eaten the last of the queen cakes, everything was all packed up and taken back to the kitchen to make a start on the sandwiches for tea.

Picnic teas were numerous sliced pans of salad, ham or beef sandwiches, scones or queen cakes and flasks of tea. If they worked late, the supper was similar.

An easier way to bring picnics is to make casseroles and transport the dinner in the large casserole dishes, wrapped in tea towels and in a box. Queen cakes double up as a dessert and are eaten with the mugs of tea. Most contractors seem to take sugar in their tea so I often put milk and sugar in the flask with the tea to save transporting them separately.

If bringing tea or supper to the field, sandwiches or Cornish pasties are the handiest – the difficulty is doing enough as they seem to devour sliced pan after sliced pan of sandwiches. When making salad sandwiches, mix chopped lettuce, tomatoes, hard-boiled eggs, salad onions and beetroot into a bowl, with a generous dollop of mayonnaise. Don't make these sandwiches too long in advance or the bread will go soggy. Baguettes are handier as they take less time to fill.

Unless the harvesting is miles away from your farm, tell the contractors to come to the house for their meals. Eating in the field might save them ten minutes but it will add hours to your workload. Value your own time and they will arrive when they are hungry!

How to make a perfect cup of tea (or mug of tay)

Town women have their fancy lattes and cappuccinos, but if a rural woman isn't capable of making a decent cup of tea in her own kitchen or at a local parish event, it will cause consternation. If your past experience of tea-making is using a single teabag in a mug or herbal teas in a pretty teacup, remember perfect farm wives have to make a *proper* pot of tea.

Source a teapot that doesn't drip, even if you have to ask the shop owners for recommendations or ask them to put water into the teapot so you can test it. A teapot that drips when it is pouring will drive you mad. Consider your teapot a serious investment for the future. It just might last you a lifetime.

Buy two teapots: one for family use, capable of making at least four mugs of tea, and a larger one for when there are contractors or visitors.

Scald the teapot by pouring in an inch of boiling water and letting it sit for at least thirty seconds. Throw that out and add the required number of teabags or teaspoons of loose tea before filling it with boiling water. Place a tea cosy on the teapot and wait two minutes for it to draw before pouring. (The tea cosy was knitted by your own fair hands of course.)

This is the conundrum – should the milk or the tea be poured in first? Historically tea was poured in first to prove the quality of the china in the teacups. Ordinary china can crack when hot liquid is poured into it, bone china does not. It's up to personal preference now.

Don't worry about making cappuccinos, lattes and coffees. It's okay for Irish farm wives to make awful coffee, but the tea must be good.

Never offer a cup of tea on its own. Whether the tea break offers the excuse of a chat or sustenance, at the very least biscuits should be served. If offering only biscuits, always apologise for the absence of home baking. This will suggest if they had called at any other time, there would have been a freshly baked cake.

Always offer a "hot drop". This is a refill but usually offered when the cup of tea is still half full.

FARM WIFE QUIZ (3)

1. It's wash day. Do you:
    (a) Separate clothes into three piles: whites, colours and farm clothes
    (b) Check all pockets and sort into piles according to the water temperature they need – whites, farm clothes, fast coloureds, minimum iron, delicate fabrics, woollens ...
    (c) Have "his and her" laundry baskets and let him do his own washing?

2. It is three days since you've seen another human being apart from the immediate family. A car drives up to the front door. Do you:
    (a) Go to the front door to have a quick chat and try to get rid of them
    (b) Think to yourself, "Who on earth is this disturbing my peace and quiet?" but be friendly when chatting to them
    (c) Throw open the front door and invite them in for tea and biscuits – it doesn't matter who they are – you'll take anybody right now?

3. The inside of the teapot needs cleaning. Do you:
   (a) Pop it in the dishwasher weekly
   (b) Pour in boiling water and two dessertspoons of bread soda and leave it the teapot for a few hours before scrubbing clean
   (c) Buy a "teapot cleaning kit" in the supermarket?

4. You are about to put his farming clothes in the washing machine. Do you:
   (a) Presume he has emptied the pockets and chuck them in
   (b) Check the pockets for miscellaneous oddments that could damage the machine, (not to mention important receipts), before pre-treating the numerous stains
   (c) Get a pair of rubber gloves and a tongs – there's no way you are touching those?

5. You have four loads of washing to do. Although it is July, it has been raining for three days. Do you:
   (a) Leave them until tomorrow, it might be dry then
   (b) Wash them and hang them out on the clothes line in the empty hay shed – you can air them over the Aga later
   (c) Wash them and dry them in the tumble dryer?

6. Is your kitchen floor:
   (a) Cream textured lino – you're fed up scrubbing it (albeit only occasionally) and you're going to change it for dark grey
   (b) Dark grey tiles and scrubbed weekly
   (c) Cream textured tiles, spotlessly clean – he isn't allowed in until he has taken a shower and changed his clothes?

7. You need milk for the breakfast but you're not dressed yet. Do you:
   (a) Pull on the wellies and run up the yard to the milk tank in your pyjamas
   (b) Get dressed and run up the yard to the milk tank
   (c) Go through your beauty routine, put on your make-up and get dressed before going to the shop for your special order of skimmed extra protein milk?

8. You are going to make brown bread but don't have any sour milk or buttermilk. Do you:
   (a) Add a teaspoon of vinegar to the milk and let it sit for ten minutes
   (b) Decide to make some butter so you'll have some buttermilk to make the brown bread
   (c) Go to the shop for a loaf of bread?

9. You have ripped a favourite cardigan. Do you:
   (a) Darn it – you're a bit rusty but it'll do
   (b) Repair it with the wool you have kept for such an eventuality since you knitted it
   (c) Send it off to be mended or put it in a bag for the charity shop?

10. What does this expression mean – "Would you like a hot drop in that?"
    (a) A drop of whisky or poitin
    (b) A refill of tea
    (c) More hot water?

How did you do?

Mostly A's – You fly by the seat of your pants at times but you're good enough to get by

Mostly B's – You are really on the ball, your mother-in-law would have to get up early to catch you out.

Mostly C's – Well, your house is spotless, even your wellies don't have a hint of mud on them.

PART FIVE

COMMUNITY SPIRIT

Is living in a small rural community "the good life"? Do people know each other well, support others in times of trouble and drop in to neighbours like a rural version of *Desperate Housewives*? Yes, there are rural communities just like that. Women call with loaves of fresh brown bread or scones if a neighbour is ill. Men call to borrow trailers, muck spreaders or mowers. Farming neighbours help each other out all the time. If someone spots livestock on the road, they'll make sure they are safe and then alert the owners. If a farmer has to stop because another is moving livestock, he or she will jump out of the car and stand in a gap if it looks like an extra body would be useful.

Years ago, people met each other at their nearest crossroads. Wooden benches were set into hedges and old men in black coats sat or stood, waving with their walking sticks at each passing car and chatting to every passerby. Women met each other at bingo and Mass and in the summer evenings when their work was done, they'd go for a walk with the intention of having a natter with someone. Young men played handball or football with other young men (but not women). Entertainment was simple. In the early 1950s, children and adults would watch out for my grand-uncle as he drove from Carlow to Garrendenny every Sunday. As he used to time himself with a stop watch in an attempt to break his record, seeing a car going so fast created huge excitement.

Nowadays, communities vary hugely in terms of how often people call into neighbours. The men usually know each other well, most grew up together and they know each other's families as well as all those skeletons in the cupboards. Some farmers call into each other's yards frequently, dropping in to borrow something and staying for a chat. Meeting places include a local shop (if there is one), church (men congregate outside after the service to discuss farming), the local pub and the local agricultural store (known in Ireland as the creamery). If it wasn't for these meeting places and the need to borrow machinery occasionally, some farmers wouldn't see anyone from one end of the week to the next. They might complain the "quick" visit to the creamery took so long due to being waylaid by other farmers, but in reality they enjoyed the chat.

As more farm wives work off farm now, it can be difficult for women, as the "blow-in", to get to know their neighbours. You won't have to introduce yourself to anyone though: they all know who you are! It is easier when kids come along as primary school drop offs and collections provide opportunities to get to know other mums. Even if you find it hard to get to know other farm women, don't expect any part of your life to remain private, it will be of immense interest to all. You might even be the hot topic of conversation occasionally!

How to get to know your neighbours

Many farm wives have moved counties or countries to live on the farm. You are bound to miss your family and friends. Skyping and Facebook aren't the same as meeting up on a regular basis. It takes time to make new friends and settle into a new community especially if you are commuting to a town or city to work. Things happen slowly in the countryside and families new to an area are considered to be "blow-ins" for at least a generation!

If your next-door (next-field) neighbours moved to the country to get away from pollution and traffic, with no farming background whatsoever, they might not be too appreciative when the contractors are trundling past their house at midnight with your silage. They may consider tractor work at weekends to be inconsiderate and spreading slurry on a bank holiday is bound to raise objections. They may not realise rain is forecast so you have to work on the bank holidays, although you'd much prefer to be at the beach. If you have neighbours like that, try and get them on side by presenting them with a housewarming gift of a homemade cake. Get their mobile numbers so you can text to notify them when the slurry will be spread so they know to change plans if they've invited friends around. However, if they are awkward, reserve the smelliest slurry for the field adjoining their back garden.

Some neighbours are great. They'll let you borrow anything you want, call to help if there's a calamity, and take care of the catering if there is a bereavement. In the past, many farmers provided elderly neighbours with a trailer load of chopped sticks every winter.

 When you move in and are welcomed into the area, take the plunge and repay their call with a visit and some home baking. If you know your husband's family visit elderly neighbours, continue the tradition by calling with half a dozen eggs or a cake. Buying produce in the local shop, attending the local church, joining the local sport club – they all help to get to know the neighbours. If you'd like to get to know them all in one fell swoop, you could host a coffee morning for charity. It's certainly one way to break the ice.

How to get involved in local community events

If you were brought up in a town or city, you probably miss the conveniences of local shops, supermarkets and cinemas. It takes time to acclimatise to having to drive a couple of miles to buy a bag of sugar, not to mention a half-hour drive for a latte. And forget about a Friday night takeaway; they don't deliver out as far as your farm. Going to town involves racing around grocery shopping and picking up parts for the farm. I'm afraid things like fitting in a treatment with the beautician or having a long lunch are in the past too!

However, there's plenty to get involved in in most rural areas. Look out for groups that you'd be interested in joining. There's bound to be sport clubs, a book club or a farming group. If you like crafts and baking, contact The Irish Countrywomen's Association as it has a number of guilds in each county. If you have children, you can get involved in the school's parents' association. Getting voted onto committees is one of the best ways of getting to know new people. But be careful, you could end up going to a meeting every night of the week.

As with all community events and committees, a tough skin is recommended before you join. Don't bother to get into "competitions" over the most impressive floral arrangements for church or the most popular tray bakes at the village fair. If you try, someone is bound to attempt to put you in your place. As I mentioned before, my one and only signature dish is my biscuit cake and it has been described as "a couple of packets of biscuits mashed up", which made me chuckle. Ironically, at another event, my biscuit cake was singled out as "the best biscuit cake" a guest speaker had ever tasted.

 Take to Twitter to chat to other women in agriculture from all over the world. You might be surprised that many of them are experiencing similar issues, and in any case there's always someone else awake on Twitter at 3am when you're up feeding a lamb.

How to help at funerals

Funerals in rural Ireland tend to be huge affairs. Apart from paying their respects to the dead, a funeral is a social occasion where attendees meet with people they haven't seen for years. The deceased was likely to be well known for decades. Everyone who knew him/her attends the wake and funeral. In addition, those who know any of his/her family members and wish to sympathise will attend too.

The Irish wake is still very much in existence. Relatives, friends and neighbours visit the family's home to express their condolences, to view the deceased and to say a prayer for their soul. While the image of the traditional Irish wake has sometimes been an alcohol-fuelled affair, they now tend to be confined to multiple cups of tea, sandwiches and cake. Every sympathiser sits at the dining or kitchen table to have a cup of tea and exchange conversation about the deceased, the weather and the state of farming with others.

It is considered polite to exchange views on how the deceased died and their appearance so expressions such as "She looks so peaceful", "He looks like he is asleep", and "Doesn't he look so young, not grey in the face at all" are repeated again and again over the two days of the wake and funeral. A lovely expression at a farmer's wake is "His/her work is done" meaning he/she worked hard and is now gone to rest. Farmers rarely like to be the centre of attention and yet, for two days, they are exactly that as hundreds of people visit.

Of course, it can also happen when the eulogy is delivered, you wonder if you are at the right funeral as virtues are extolled and you don't recognise any of them. Even if the deceased was a miserable old sod, people never speak ill of the dead – not publicly anyway. They become a saint as soon as they stop breathing, at least for the duration of the wake and funeral.

Farming communities have a stoical view when a person dies of old age. If the deceased had a good life, that is mentioned again and again. In many ways, the wake and funeral act to celebrate his or her life; don't be surprised when laughter rings out as people tell funny stories from the past. However, if it is a tragic death, shock resonates through the whole community.

 A competent farm wife would never consider visiting a wake without bringing something with her. That something is usually a tray of sandwiches, a platter of buttered scones or a homemade cake. Therefore, when you hear of a bereavement locally, it's a cue to start baking. If you are a neighbour of the deceased, you might stay for hours at their kitchen sink to wash hundreds of cups and saucers. You'll agree with all the comments about how well the deceased looks and reveal (in whispers) how the rest of the family are holding up.

How to talk about the weather
- at length

For obvious reasons, the weather is always hugely important in farming. When opening a conversation, etiquette dictates the weather is given its due consideration. First you must assess the current weather conditions, then draw attention to the more dramatic weather patterns over the previous week, and once that has been done to death can you both attempt to predict the weather for the next week. Here's an example of the first few lines to get you started:

"How are ye? Grand day, thank God."

"It is, fierce heat altogether, I was nearly melted yesterday."

"Ah, it was a grand day, herself brought the chaps to the beach and said it was windy enough down there."

"I suppose it would be. Did ye hear about the flash floods last Monday?"

"Aye, I did and they say it is to rain heavy at the end of the week."

"Sure, everyone has their hay done now, we could do with the sup of rain."

If asking someone for something, it is considered too rude to ask outright; first you must make small talk which means more conversation about the weather. Even if you are in a hurry, you must chat about the different types of rain that fell recently and how it affected your farm. Only when you are content responding to a conversation about the weather for ten minutes can you be considered a true Irish farm wife.

Never contradict anyone on their statements on the weather. Just reply automatically with "Yes, it's a grand day".

How to get the farmer to attend weddings and other functions

It can be difficult to persuade a farmer to attend a wedding. They take up a lot of time. Between the travelling time to get there, the afternoon and evening of the wedding and also the next morning if you stay overnight, a wedding can take a couple of days out of your farming calendar. He thinks he gives them too much time, but he doesn't have to go shopping for an outfit, get his hair done or get a fake tan to blend in with his farmer's tan. If he goes to the barber and gets you to pick up a new shirt and tie, that's about it.

There's also the stress of having to RSVP by an appointed date. Trying to get a yes out of a farmer is impossible. You usually reply that you'll be there and he will be there if it rains – not very helpful to someone trying to do a seating plan, you just might receive a stony silence.

Many people are now having farm weddings where the reception (and sometimes the service too) are held on the farm. If the farmer sees it as an opportunity to get a good look at someone else's stock and crops, it might make it easier to get him there.

If the wedding is taking place within thirty minutes' drive, you can both go to the service and nip home for a couple of hours to milk the cows before heading back to the hotel in time for the meal. You miss only the standing around while the photographs are being taken. Alternatively, he can give the church a miss and arrive at the hotel in time for the reception.

If he isn't going and you're a little nervous about going on your own, arrive early as that's easier than walking into a full church alone. You might even find another farmer's wife there on her own.

FARM WIFE QUIZ (4)

1. You're going to a hunt ball. You have eventually found the perfect dress. It only needs:
   (a) Something to cover your shoulders as you know the fake tan will never blend in with your "farmer's tan"
   (b) Fake tan; you've been using sun block all summer
   (c) Just new shoes, new bag, new jewellery?

2. You've moved into the area and you don't know anyone. Do you:
   (a) Join the local farming groups, volunteer to go on local committees and find yourself serving up tea and cake at local fundraisers within a month
   (b) Take to Twitter to see if there are any other farmers' wives in your area – it's easier to get to know them online first
   (c) Head back to the city twice a week to meet up with friends?

3. Your neighbours phone you. They are having a birthday party for one of their children and two of your animals keep having sex in the field adjoining their garden. Do you:

   (a) Say you'll move them to another field and collapse with laughter once you say goodbye

   (b) Say that is what happens on a farm in the countryside and there's nothing you can do about it

   (c) Suggest they throw a bucket of cold water over them?

4. You arrive at a parish event. Someone else has baked the same "signature bake" as you. It might even be the same recipe. This is the parish equivalent of wearing the same dresses to a wedding. Do you:

   (a) Put your bake at the other end of the table and deliberately take a slice of hers to taste it

   (b) Put it on the table beside hers – let the public decide which one to eat and let the best one win

   (c) Bring your bake back out to the car?

5. You are sitting in the loader having raised your dearest beloved up in the bucket to clean out the guttering. While he's up there, do you:

   (a) Discuss which calves you're going to genotype this year

   (b) Remind him about the wedding you're both invited to the following Saturday and he'd better come or you'll leave him up in the air for the night

   (c) Tell him about the designer dress and shoes you've bought for the upcoming wedding?

6. It's harvesting time and you've scarcely seen him for three days. You're bringing the dinner to the field and he's stopping for a mere ten minutes to eat. Do you:

   (a) Go and drive the combine for a while to give him a break

   (b) Go and sit on the tractor with him for a chat

   (c) Get some friends around for the evening for a girly night in?

7. He phones (ten minutes before you're about to serve up dinner) to say there are three more men for dinner. Do you:

   (a) Remain calm – you had planned to freeze some of the leftovers anyway so there will be plenty

   (b) Start to work out how you can stretch that relatively small roast chicken – adding a rasher to each plate might do it

   (c) Slam down the phone?

How did you do?

Mostly A's – You're well able to deal with anything that crops up on the farm and in the locality. Well done. Perfection indeed.

Mostly B's – You're just about there as a perfect farm wife.

Mostly C's – You're definitely learning, still a little room for improvement, but getting there.

PART SIX

MANAGING MONEY AND STARTING A FARM BUSINESS

Fifty years ago and beyond, many farming families had little money but produced most of their own food. There's wasn't money for fancy clothes and most children went barefoot during the summer. Hence, there was huge excitement when a package arrived from relatives in the States, knowing it would contain gifts of clothes and playthings. Only those with relatives in the States owned denim jeans! Every person in a farming family had to pull their weight to contribute to the family income.

The 1930s was a particularly tough decade for Irish farming families. As a result of the Economic War, Britain taxed all Irish cattle entering the British market; de Valera retaliated by taxing all British imports. Farmers had no market for their beef having been reliant on the British market and exporting 750,000 head each year. However, de Valera seemed to think Ireland's non supply of beef was capable of "starving Britain" so he came up with a scheme to ensure the cattle wouldn't be sold. The government paid nine shillings and sixpence for each "clean" calf skin so farmers slaughtered their calves.[38]

Unfortunately, this scheme of trying to starve Britain backfired. Land values fell, the value of cattle slumped. Farmers still had to pay land annuities from a diminishing income.

Estate owners left the area or emigrated. Farmyards were dismal places between the absence of young calves and the stench of piled-up calf carcasses awaiting burial. The government was doing its best to emphasise the ideal of a self-sufficient, healthy and happy rural Ireland, where its people didn't need the material wealth required by those in industrial cities. However, the happy maidens dancing at the crossroads didn't quite materialise. Many complaints came from farm wives writing letters to the editors in national newspapers.

Irish Independent January 24 1939

Sir, I am sending this SOS out to every farmer in Eire to do his bit in the final struggle for immediate relief. As a farmer's wife with a large family to look after, I know that unless relief comes quickly, my own particular case will cry out for help. My children are ill-fed, badly clothed – barely shod, so badly that I cannot send them to school or even to Holy Mass.

My husband and I and our suffering children have worked under conditions that no human being should be asked in a Christian Age.

Our tortured minds, day and night, are a nightmare and the pinched, lonely and sad faces of our little ones send a shudder to our souls. Wake up. Women of the Countryside, and let us call Help Help Help.

From a Farmer's Wife

Irish Independent October 10 1939

Letter to Editor

Sir, I wonder if our government have ever given a thought as to what the life of a farmer's wife in this country at present is. We belong to the most harassed of all class of Irish farmer – the upper class on 200 acres. We pay enormous rates and workmen's wages are high. In order to meet our obligations, mine is an all time job rising at 6:30 and working till 9pm. I boil, shop, mix pig's food, have all ready for men …

I am 65 and have not much hope of rest. The way the government could best help is by de-rating for farmers.

Could they not do it by putting a tax, say of 2/6 on bicycles. No one would feel that much and they could relieve the rates out of the very large return. Why not?

A Farmer's Tired Wife

While it was possible for these women to be vocal in their complaints, one wonders how the poorer classes fared. I doubt the "high workman's wages" seemed so high to the workman themselves, and in any case they probably decreased when cattle prices slumped. It's interesting that one writer emphasised the inability to attend Mass, thereby appealing to the religious sensibility at the time.

Eighty years on, there are still challenges in farming: financial, practical, keeping up with the amount of paperwork, trying to balance the good and bad years, and inclement weather. Here are some tips for keeping things in order.

How to manage the paperwork

Farming isn't just about keeping animals fed, harvesting crops and driving around in large machinery. There is so much paperwork, you might expect that a stroll across the fields requires to be recorded in some book or app.

The Department of Agriculture has to be notified when animals are born, sold or die. Using a farming software package and their online resources make it much quicker but it still has to be done. All medicines purchased and administered have to be recorded. The purchase of all feed and fertiliser must be documented. The safety statement has to be kept up to date, safety courses must be completed and records kept of all sprays purchased and used. You also have to record it if you export slurry to another farm. Don't put your paperwork "on the long finger" as an inspector can arrive in the yard unannounced and demand to see all records. If they aren't up to date, fines are imposed. If the inspector asks when you last sneezed, don't be surprised and give the question due consideration.

Each bovine has an official passport known as a "blue card", which is, er, blue. You would think keeping all the blue cards in numerical order in a safe place would be easy wouldn't you? We keep all ours in a drawer in the kitchen dresser, which should be considered organised and safe. A few cards occasionally make their way to the kitchen table and mingle with the general chaos of newspapers, opened and unopened post, magazines and a bowl of fruit.

In the early spring of 2014, factories were very slow to take bulls and we were looking forward to each load being dispatched. One evening, I was looking for blue cards for the fifteen bulls going to the factory the next morning but I could find only twelve. The bulls were sorted and ready to go. We spent ninety minutes looking for those three cards. I checked the recycling, we both checked through the 300-odd cards, cleared off the kitchen table, filed every piece of paperwork, and pulled out drawers to check behind them. It was only when a drawer was pulled out fully and put on the floor that we noticed a card peeping up from the cupboard below. The drawer was so full, the top three cards had skimmed off the top, fallen behind and down into the cupboard. Cue a big mug of tea and a large bar of chocolate at 11:30pm!

Get a smartphone each and buy suitable management apps so that information inputted on the phone syncs to the laptop. Inputting information straight onto the tablet or smartphone saves you having to interpret scribbles on scraps of stained paper and cardboard.

How to organise your filing system

In an ideal world, you have a farm office. All farm post should be left on the desk and one morning a week, you sit down at the computer to ensure the paperwork is up to date. All post is dealt with, payments made and invoices filed. Bank statements are checked to prevent any financial surprises. Paperwork is collected by the accountant bi-monthly and the profit monitor is completed each January.

Paperwork is not piled at the end of the kitchen table, overflowing so some falls to the floor. The family isn't crammed together at meal times at one end of the table while the paperwork spreads out over the other half. Spare chairs are not used to store newspapers, farm magazines and unopened bills. Forms that are important are not left to mingle with school newsletters, the newspapers and junk mail.

If you don't have a farm office, put it on the wishlist. Until then, invite visitors regularly. Tidying up for visitors means the kitchen table doesn't get out of control.

How to keep control of cash flow

According to Teagasc (the agriculture and food development authority in Ireland), one-third of Irish farms in 2014 were not viable. That means more money could be going out than coming in. If you want it to pay you a salary, you need to know which enterprises are making money and which are costing you.

Receipts and invoices must be retained and filed (ideally in a lever arch file or at worst, in a shoebox). Efficient bookkeeping starts with rescuing receipts from the pockets of farm clothes before they make it into the washing machine. Yes, they will be stained with dubious substances. You might want to wear gloves.

Many farmers are so busy doing the farming that they don't have time to sit down and work out which enterprises are the most profitable. By getting involved, you will know what is going on and make sound business decisions. You can work as a couple to keep in the black for the majority of the year ... or at least not as far into the red as it might be if you didn't keep on top of things.

As with many self-employed small businesses, cash flow can be an issue. The issue being there is money going out every month and at times no money coming in. Between the mortgage, farm loans, machinery repayments, insurance, feed and fertiliser, contractors and staff, vets and medicines, chocolate biscuits and new wellies, not to mention your salary ... yes, your eyes will water and your heart flutter. It is also a surprise when your accountant calculates a significant tax bill for the farm– surely they must have been looking at a different set of bank statements!

A perfect farm wife, together with the farmer, is good at money management and budgets for the year. You estimate the income and outgoings for each month and plan accordingly. Never should the bank manager receive an emergency phone call asking them to extend the overdraft or should they have to phone you to ask when will money be going into the account.

You might need to keep a tight rein on your farmer too as they like their machinery. It is not unknown to hear him moan at your new pair of shoes only to head off to an agricultural show, returning in the evening with one cheque missing from the cheque book. News of a new piece of machinery arriving and a sizeable hole in the bank account means that you are owed one heck of a lot of shoes.

 Having a second source of income on the farm is valued and that's where you come in. It means there is a "Peter" who can be robbed to pay "Paul"!

How to stay on good terms with the bank manager

Love them or hate them, banks are essential. If you were accustomed to receiving the same salary every month with an occasional bonus and you give up work, it can be hard to adjust to the flux of farming income, with no income at all for some months. You need to stay on good terms with your bank manager for any emergency requests.

You might think the bank is delighted to lend you money as you have the assets of the farm behind you. After all, they are probably rubbing their hands with glee with all that interest they will rake in. That might be the case, but they won't make their generosity or their glee too obvious. Indeed, they act like they are doing you the favour and may even make you sweat before saying yes to your requests. Learning how to negotiate with a bank manager is a useful skill. Gone are the days when you could fight hard for a good interest rate as the central office makes these decisions now, but it is still worth giving it your all.

It is a good idea to listen carefully to the bank manager when he rings. Brian was working away in a windswept field one day when the phone rang. The bank manager wanted to tell him that our bank account was so red it was scarlet, but Brian couldn't hear him properly. Brian thought he said we were a couple of hundred over so was quite relaxed and told him it would be fine, I'd put a cheque in and he was selling another load of cattle within days. We got another call the next day, and the bank manager was insistent this time. It turned out we were still overdrawn by thousands. I had lodged the cheque for €17,000 into the credit card account instead of the current account, using the wrong card by mistake. It took two weeks to get the funds transferred!

Competent farm wives would never make that mistake, would they?

Another way to impress a bank manager is with your qualifications, if you have letters after your name. Brian had a pound sterling account with an Irish bank and wanted to close it and remove the remaining funds. On the way home from an appointment, he called to a branch of the bank (but not the branch we deal with). While waiting to be served, a bank manager took a quick look at his letter and said someone would be with him shortly. Then he changed his tune and ushered Brian into his office. The bank manager was filling out the relevant forms and chatting away. Brian was nonplussed at this sudden favourable treatment. He realised why when asked, "Are you practising out in Crettyard?"

"Practising? Hmmm, no."

"Where are you practising now then?"

"Oh, I see. Ah, I'm a farmer."

They then had to make polite conversation about the advantages in changing careers while the manager finished the form. The cows may not appreciate a PhD in microbiology but the occasional person is impressed by it. Brian had totally forgotten the letter addressed him as Dr. I guess farmers just aren't as illustrious as GPs.

Bank managers are akin to well-trained husbands. They are calm if they know money is forthcoming, just like husbands relax if they know dinner is on the way. In both instances, good communication is key.

How to forge your husband's signature (allegedly)

Most farmers' wives end up "imitating" their husband's signature sooner rather than later. If a form needs to be signed and he isn't around, it is easier to forge his signature than go on a wild goose chase looking for him.

Technically, of course, this is fraud. But this is Ireland where such technicalities tend to be overlooked when it is between husband and wife and it prevents arguments. As we each have herd numbers, cheques are made out to one or other of us. I always forget to ask Brian to sign the back of his cheques before I go to the bank. Bank cashiers usually tell me to go and get it signed before I can pay it in. I was amused one day when a cashier said "Put Brian's signature on the back of that". I couldn't possibly comment on whether I was able to do this.

A rep once told me that a farmer's wife had been signing her husband's cheques for so long that if the farmer actually signed one himself the bank would probably return it as being forged.

Get him to adopt a squiggle for his signature as this should make it much easier. Not that I have tried it out.

How to bring in additional income

Family farms are the norm in Ireland, but not all of them can support a family financially without another income. Most farms needed additional income in the past too. Women's income was usually described as "pin money", which suggests it was extra pocket money, small amounts to spend on treats or days out. That wasn't the case at all.

Many farm women kept hens and sold their eggs at weekly markets or to neighbours. Forty chickens were equal to a cow in value[39] and many had well over a hundred hens. Women used their egg money to contribute to the weekly rent, barter for groceries and save for clothing. Farm women were resourceful. The demand for eggs increased before Christmas and supply decreased as hens don't produce as many when it gets dark and cold. From September onwards, many stored some eggs in a glycerine liquid to extend their freshness. Those eggs were used in their own pre-Christmas baking so all available fresh eggs were sold for higher prices in November and December.

A laying hen was never killed for meat but once they stopped laying, they were swiftly dispatched with a wring of the neck and prepared for the pot. They were boiled in water and a few vegetables to make a soup and the boiled hen was then roasted in the oven to create what was, apparently, a tender and tasty meal. Not a scrap was wasted.

Keeping hens wasn't just a case of tossing them some corn in a picturesque farmyard and collecting the eggs. Potatoes and barley or oats were boiled (water had to be carried and potatoes dug), houses were bedded with clean straw regularly, eggs had to be washed, graded and sold. Many kept turkeys and geese for the Christmas market too. From the 1920s, the hard work of poultry keeping was recognised in sayings such as "good luck and lazy poultrywomen are strangers", and "like the housewife, the henwife's work is never done".[40]

Women also took in sewing, knitting or embroidery work from agents. These home industries were supported as they conformed to an idealised image of women in the home. Married women working outside the home faced disapproval. It didn't matter that women worked all hours as long as it wasn't in public.[41] Home working wasn't limited to the wives of agricultural labourers and tenant farmers or to single women: the wives of relatively well-off farmers were doing it too.

Nowadays, with the increase in house building on the farm (as the young married couple almost always build or renovate a house for themselves on the farm), there's also an increase in mortgages. More income is needed to keep two vehicles, pay the mortgage, purchase machinery, invest in farm improvements, fund retirements and pay for holidays, and that is why a second income is required in most farm households. It is a rare farmer's wife who can manage to be a "lady who lunches".

Having a career in teaching is the "laying hen" as far as farming is concerned. You're working when the children are in school and off when they are on holidays. Apart from saving on childcare, you're available to stop gaps, cook for contractors and bring in the hay. When I was judging the Blue Jean Country Queen Festival[42] last year, I was amused that many of the contenders were either teachers or in teacher training – wonderful farm partner potential.

What if you want to set up a business on the farm? Many women have started businesses from "the kitchen table" in order to put children through university and they have grown to be more profitable than the farm. Other reasons include needing something to feed your brain cells, or you've realised waiting for the farm to pay for a new kitchen is going to take decades. The farm can be a perfect setting for a home-based business and you never know where it might lead you.

Farm business ideas

Adding value to produce

Farmhouse cheese, yoghurts and cheesecakes

Are you fed up with the fluctuating milk price? Are you precise when baking? Do you love cheese? Do you enjoy meeting people at farmers' markets? Only if you answer yes to all of these questions should you attempt to make cheese! If you're the type of person who guesses at measurements when baking cakes or isn't keen on chatting to strangers for long, it's probably not the best choice of business for you.

The number of farmhouse cheeses being produced and winning global prizes might suggest it is a flooded market, but there's always room for another good cheese.

It's worth considering yoghurt or cheesecake making too. The world's your oyster when it comes to creating delicious food with dairy products.

Jam making

Lots of people don't attempt to make jam but love to buy it homemade. Start off by making extra pots of jam for family and friends. If they praise it, try selling some in a local shop or at a farmer's market. Grow the enterprise slowly and see where it takes you.

Fruit and vegetables

Have you a flair for growing fruit and vegetables? Do you find you have surplus every year and you're giving them away? Start off by bartering or selling them on a small scale and spread your reputation. Depending on your location, you can sell at a farmers' market, open a farm shop or offer classes in growing vegetables.

Eggs

Many of our predecessors had successful poultry businesses. Hens and ducks don't need a huge investment to get started. Selling free-range eggs from the farm gate with an honesty box doesn't take much investment, yet selling even twenty dozen eggs per week can add a small regular income when kids are small. The biggest threat might be Mr Fox, so invest in a dog and good fencing.

Selling meat direct to market

Are your animals special in any way? Are they a particularly popular breed, is their meat special or are they organic? Selling meat direct to the consumer is a lot of work but the margin is greatly increased. A product like free-range chicken or duck will often be in demand with consumers and with restaurants.

Woollen products

If you arc fcd up that the price received for the sheep's wool is only slightly more than the cost of shearing it, it's time to work out how you can add value to it. Are your sheep rare? Is there something distinctive about their fleece? Blankets from Irish Zwartbles sheep are now making their way around the world from their origin in Co. Kilkenny. Can you create your own line of wool from the fleeces and knit your own products?

Tourism

There's been increased interest recently in farming, not just from city dwellers but also from farmers worldwide wanting to visit farms in other countries. From farm tours to food trails to opening farms on Sundays, visiting a farm is the new black as far as days out and holidays are concerned.

Accommodation

There's little point trying to compete with the hotel deals for their luxury accommodation, spas and swimming pools, but consider targeting those wanting to stay on a working farm. If you have a couple of spare en-suite bedrooms and you like chatting to people, cooking and having the house in tip-top condition, you can benefit from keeping the house spick and span and offer accommodation. Let your visitors collect eggs and see the cows being milked. With the growth in popularity for Airbnb, it is much easier to get started on a relatively informal basis.

Offering glamping or camping is another type of accommodation to consider. Promote it by sharing photographs of your surroundings on the various social media platforms – not forgetting to take selfies with your animals.

Using your existing facilities

What do you have an interest in that is also attractive to visitors? Can you piggyback on any attractions nearby? If your farm is passed by tourists on the way to a nearby attraction, a tea rooms or farm shop could become very busy. It could also be used for occasional baking or cookery classes. With the increase in traffic, cycle trails and walking paths are proving attractive.

I love hearing about farm businesses offering team-building workshops to corporate businesses, letting them compete in teams to bring in turf with a stubborn donkey or rounding up wild sheep without the help of a dog.

Remember you have to like working with the general public though, there's no point setting up this type of business if you are more of a grumpy hermit.

Crafts

Are you a crafter? If you are good with your hands and have an eye for good design, whether it is crochet, knitwear, jewellery or paper crafts, you don't even have to go to country markets to sell nor invest in an ecommerce website. You can sell on websites like Etsy, NotOnTheHighStreet or eBay. They act as your shop window and take a small percentage from sales. These sites are accessed from all over the world, so whether you feel like clicking those knitting needles or making jewellery or sculpture, as long as the photographs are good, you have a sellable product.

Weddings

Most people spend a lot of money on their wedding. Can you target brides and grooms with your farm?

Farm weddings

The romance of farmhouse weddings is growing but you do need a handsome barn that is level and clean and can be "prettied" up. You also need ample parking and an attractive small field or large garden if they want to have the wedding outdoors. Can you see your farm as a wedding destination? If you are already running a B&B and providing meals, it would be a complementary add-on.

Again, you need to have excellent people skills as you're bound to be dealing with a couple of bridezillas and their mothers in the year.

Hen parties

Now that you are a perfect farm wife, you can pass on your skills. If the bride is marrying a farmer, she and her friends can have great fun learning how to become great farm wives. Show them how to make brown bread, milk a goat, round up some sheep, throw wellies and collect eggs.

Other ideas

Work to your skills and amenities, but you might think about:

- Educational workshops for children
- Setting up an open farm
- Designing stationery and products with agricultural themes
- Using the land to host a festival
- Providing space for a writing retreat
- Making specialist cakes or cake toppers
- Training sheepdogs
- Grooming animals for shows (those hairdressing skills again)
- Farm secretarial/bookkeeping services
- Starting a micro-brewery.

Pick something you enjoy and develop it into a business.

Tips for setting up a business

Here are a few things to think about:

- Start small and inexpensively. Use that kitchen table for yet another purpose.
- See if there are any grants available. If you don't ask, you won't get.
- Can you get a mentor?
- Write a list of questions and find people who can answer them. Can you learn from similar businesses?
- If you are turning your hobby into a business, decide if you will still love it when you are spending multiple hours at it every day?
- Get sound advice from professionals – the bank, an accountant, a solicitor, the Revenue, an insurance specialist, your local enterprise agency, the Chamber of Commerce.
- Network – online and offline. Tell people about your business.
- Start a blog to attract your target market.
- Start using social media channels to benefit your business and give you access to consumers. Choose from Twitter, Facebook, Pinterest, LinkedIn and Instagram.
- Write a business plan. Identify your strengths and weaknesses, as well as the opportunities and threats for your business.
- Research your target market. Who is he/she? Where are they based? What is their income? What age are they? Are they married or single? Do they have surplus money to buy your product? Is your product considered a necessity or an extravagance?
- Who are your competitors? How can you be better than them?

FARM WIFE QUIZ (5)

1. The accountant is looking for some missing details for the year's accounts. Do you:
    (a) Check through the files and find them within 30 seconds
    (b) Contact your bookkeeper as she has all the files (receipts in a shoebox)
    (c) Have to spend an hour going through a box of miscellaneous papers and receipts?

2. The price of your farm product (milk, beef, lamb) hits an all-time low this year. Do you:
    (a) Shrug and say "at least there will be less going to the tax office", plus your new business is bringing in an income now
    (b) Resolve to spend a bit less on shoes this year
    (c) Curse the day that you married a farmer?

3. You've joined the ICA/WI and discovered your talent for knitting and creating patterns has been re-awakened. Do you:
    (a) Resolve to set up a business
    (b) Decide to test your skills against others by entering relevant classes in agricultural shows
    (c) Knit beautiful cashmere cardigans for all your friends?

4. You arrive at the bank and realise your husband hasn't signed the back of his cheques. Do you:
   (a) Forge his signature and pay them in via the machine
   (b) Return home to get him to sign them
   (c) Pay them in anyway; you got away with it the last time?

5. Visitors arrive unexpectedly. Which room do you usher them into?
   (a) The sitting room, it might be a bit chilly but at least it's tidy and you've just baked scones so they can have afternoon tea in there
   (b) You talk to them at the hall door, hoping they get the message that you're busy (and the house is a mess) and they will disappear
   (c) The kitchen, it's always spotless and you bought some chocolate biscuits too.

How did you do?

Mostly A's – You're positive, efficient and determined with plenty of business acumen. Well done.

Mostly B's – Hmmm, maybe you need to improve on your time management.

Mostly C's – I'm not convinced you're business-minded but your farmhouse is beautiful and you're always dressed impeccably.

CONCLUSION

Farm wives, past and present, have been appreciated by farmers, journalists and politicians. This quote from Minister Haughey (in 1964, but just as relevant today) emphasises the importance of women in a farming relationship:

> The wife is just as important in farming as the husband. Our farms are true family enterprises, joint enterprises. On the decisions made jointly by husband and wife, progress really depends.[43]

Even if your husband doesn't say so, he needs you by his side.

If you read the job description, you might have been overwhelmed but you have mastered every aspect of it. You nurture your own kids as well as the livestock. You care for your husband who occasionally needs a shoulder to lean on and someone to shout at as well as an adviser and a nurse. You're able to adjust quickly when requests for meals alter in type, time and number. You know that when you get a request to help for "a minute", it could be hours later when you return to the cake you were baking or the paperwork you were wrangling with. You might have planned a day in town buying clothes for an upcoming event but end up running for spare parts and bringing dinners to the field. You're capable of understanding his monosyllabic grunts and yes, his instructions too.

You're never "just a farmer's wife". You're pretty darn incredible.

Farming can be a tough business in a world of uncertainty and there will be good years and bad years, good days and bad days. There will be times when you'll just want to cry and there will be days when you feel your heart could burst with pride and happiness. Look to your predecessors for inspiration and be satisfied with your own efforts. Never forget to celebrate your achievements too.

The advantages of living on a farm are many: you're never bored; you are your own boss; you see beautiful and ever-changing views every day; you don't have to commute to work; you don't have to dress up or wear make-up if you don't want to, and the rural lifestyle is a great upbringing for your children. You work with your best friend on a daily basis (even though you sometimes might feel like prodding him with a pitchfork). Never forget what made you fall in love with him in the first place. He may work all hours but there will be days when he stops working to watch a beautiful sunset with you or he brings you a bunch of wild flowers. Don't lose your sense of humour. Prepare for the worst and it won't be too bad.

Tell each other your dreams for the farm, and together you will work out how to get there.

I Now Pronounce You A <u>Perfect</u> Farm Wife

FOLLOW ME ON SOCIAL MEDIA

I hope you enjoyed reading *How To Be A Perfect Farm Wife* and if you would like to follow my farm life on my blog, do visit it at www.irishfarmerette.com.

I'm also on Twitter @IrishFarmerette and @LornaSixsmith, Instagram as @IrishFarmerette, Facebook at /IrishFarmerette and Pinterest as @LornaSixsmith. I'd love to hear what you thought of the book and whether you recognised your own situation. I'd also love to hear about your own farming life, so do pop along to your favourite social media platform and say hi.

The hashtag is #perfectfarmwife if you'd like to join in any online conversations about the book.

If you haven't read it yet, I hope you now feel tempted to get my first book *Would You Marry A Farmer?* and that you enjoy it when you do.

FURTHER READING

I have cited a number of books in the notes, but I've also consulted more that you might be interested in. Here's a suggested list and do visit my website www.irishfarmerette.com for more suggestions.

Irish farming history

The Irish Countrywomen's Association, A History 1910–2000, Aileen Heverin.

A History of Irish Farming 1750–1950; *Rooted in the Soil* and *Irish Farming Life*, Jonathan Bell and Mervyn Watson.

Agriculture and Settlement in Ireland, edited by Margaret Murphy and Matthew Stout.

Ireland's Arctic Siege: The Big Freeze of 1947, Kevin C. Kearns.

Irish women's history

Unmanageable Revolutionaries, Margaret Ward.

Irish Women and Irish Migration, edited by Patrick O'Sullivan.

Culture and Society in Ireland Since 1750, edited by John Cunningham and Niall O'Ciosain.

www.modernwifemodernlifeexhibition.com (book forthcoming), Ciara Meehan.

Farm memoirs

Breakfast The Night Before, Marjorie Quarton.
A Year on Our Farm, Ann and Robin Talbot.
The Lie of the Land, P. J. Cunningham.
Any Fool Can Be a Dairy Farmer, James Robertson.
Worse Could Have Happened, Andrew D. Forrest.
To School Through the Fields, Alice Taylor.
The Yorkshire Shepherdess, Amanda Owen.
Over the Farmer's Gate, Roger Evans.

Business books

Not Enough Hours, Owen Fitzpatrick.
Money for Jam, Oonagh Monahan.
And of course, my ebook with Amanda Webb *365 Social Media Tips*; you'll find it on Amazon.

NOTES

[1] A dowry was a financial settlement made by a bride's family to her new husband (or his parents). The size of the dowry was usually determined by the value of the farm she was marrying into.

[2] *Irish Press* 5th July 1947 p6

[3] Morton, H. V. *In Search of Ireland* (Metheun, 1930, this edition 1984) p187

[4] Bourke, Joanna, *Husbandry to Housewifery: Women, Economic Change, and Housework in Ireland 1890–1914* (Oxford University Press, 1993) p13

[5] Sayers, Peig, *Peig: The Autobiography of Peig Sayers of the Great Blasket Island* (Dublin, 1973)

[6] Bell, Jonathan and Watson, Mervyn, *Irish Farming Life* (Four Courts Press, 2014) p24

[7] *The Irish Times* 27 July 2015, "What was on Irish women's minds in the 1960s?" by Caitriona Clear

[8] Research presented by William Smyth of University College Cork, Teagasc conference, May 2014

[9] Fencing refers to putting up fences with wire, stakes, hammer and staples (not the sport).

[10] Movember refers to the charity work every November when men are sponsored to grow a moustache. Farmers tend to go for the unshaven, rather ungroomed, look at busy times of the year.

[11] Bell and Watson, pp139–145

[12] From the 1930s to 1973 women had to give up their public service jobs when they married. When Ireland entered the EEC, the government had to remove the "marriage bar". Women were free to continue working if they wished, although they could avail of a tax-free bonus if they gave up work within two years of marriage.

[13] Heverin, Aileen, *The Irish Countrywomen's Association, A History 1910–2000* (Wolfhound Press, 2000) p150

[14] *Glenroe* was an Irish soap opera that was shown on Sunday nights from 8:30–9:00. It was hugely popular in the 1980s.

[15] Heverin, p31

[16] Heverin, p100

[17] http://www.snopes.com/history/document/sewing.asp

[18] *The Irish Times* 27 July 2015, "What was on Irish women's minds in the 1960s?" by Caitriona Clear

[19] *Irish Press* 28 November 1968

[20] From an interview with Eimer, born in 1942. O'Carroll, Ide B. *Models for Movers, Irish Women's Emigration to America* (Attic Press, first published 1990, now twenty-fifth anniversary edition 2015) p82

[21] Irish Rural Network report on "Women in Agriculture" by Lily Mulhall and Pat Bogue, December 1913

[22] Shortall, Sally, "Gender, Power and Farming: Northern Ireland, Canada and Norway Compared" in Byrne, Anne and Leonard, Madeleine eds *Women in Irish Society: A Sociological Reader* (Beyond the Pale Publications 1997) p396

[23] Bourke, p27

[24] *Irish Independent* 1 August 1995, p31

[25] Irish Heart Foundation, research published on 19 May 1915 http://www.irishheart.ie/iopen24/farmers-high-risk-heart-disease-stroke-n-504.html

[26] *Irish Independent* 20 January 2009

[27] Daly, Willie, *The Last Matchmaker* (Sphere, 2010) p128

[28] *Rural Life, in the Management of Horses, Dogs, Cattle, Sheep, Pigs and Poultry* (The London Printing and Publishing Co Ltd 1860) p669

[29] Father Jack was the alcoholic retired priest in the popular TV programme *Father Ted*. He was a man of few words; two of them were "Feck" and "Drink".

[30] *Rural Life*, p681

[31] *Rural Life*, p682

[32] *The Kerryman* 11 May 1979

[33] Sweeney, Frank, "It's the Milkman!" *History Ireland*, January/February 2010, Volume 18

[34] Heverin, p106

[35] *Irish Independent*, "Rolling Back The Years 1960–1964" supplement, 8 October 2011, p11

[36] A tray bake is any baked item that can be served singly and eaten without the need for a plate and fork. "Finger food" that is sweet rather than savoury.

[37] Modern Wife Modern Life exhibition, National Print Museum Dublin, July–August 2015, curated by Ciara Meehan

[38] Forrest, Andrew D, *Worse Could Have Happened* (Poolbeg Press, 1999) p179

[39] Bell and Watson, p42

[40] Bourke, p196

[41] Holmes, Janice and Urquhart, Diane (eds) *Coming into the Light: The Work, Politics and Religion of Women in Ulster 1840-1940* (Queens University, 1994), p11

[42] Macra na Feirme (a young farmers group) has many festivals during the year. The Blue Jean Country Queen is organised by Co. Meath Macra na Feirme. Representatives from branches all over the country compete to win the title each year.

[43] *Tuam Herald* 28 August 1964

Printed in Poland
by Amazon Fulfillment
Poland Sp. z o.o., Wrocław

65861241R00148